What readers are saying about
tmux: Productive Mouse-Free Development

As a tmux beginner, this book lowered the barrier of entry and made me more productive. By the time I got to the end of the book I felt like a tmux veteran.

➤ **Jeff Carley**
   Senior software engineer, Getty Images

Brian's book serves as an excellent introduction for those among us who've heard about tmux but have never quite been sure where to start. Well written and straight to the point, it'll help answer all those basic questions you have about tmux in an easy to follow format.

➤ **Darcy Laycock**
   Software engineer, Filter Squad

I've often watched over the shoulders of terminal power users with envy. *tmux: Productive Mouse-Free Development* has put me on the path to being one of those users.

➤ **Luke Chadwick**
   @vertis

tmux

Productive Mouse-Free Development

Brian P. Hogan

The Pragmatic Bookshelf

Dallas, Texas • Raleigh, North Carolina

Many of the designations used by manufacturers and sellers to distinguish their products are claimed as trademarks. Where those designations appear in this book, and The Pragmatic Programmers, LLC was aware of a trademark claim, the designations have been printed in initial capital letters or in all capitals. The Pragmatic Starter Kit, The Pragmatic Programmer, Pragmatic Programming, Pragmatic Bookshelf, PragProg and the linking *g* device are trademarks of The Pragmatic Programmers, LLC.

Every precaution was taken in the preparation of this book. However, the publisher assumes no responsibility for errors or omissions, or for damages that may result from the use of information (including program listings) contained herein.

Our Pragmatic courses, workshops, and other products can help you and your team create better software and have more fun. For more information, as well as the latest Pragmatic titles, please visit us at *http://pragprog.com*.

The team that produced this book includes:

Susannah Pfalzer (editor)
David J Kelly (typesetter)
Janet Furlow (producer)
Juliet Benda (rights)
Ellie Callahan (support)

Printed in the United States of America.
ISBN-13: 978-1-934356-96-8
Printed on acid-free paper.
Book version: P3.0—March 2014

Contents

Acknowledgments

This book started out as something I'd planned to self-publish, but working with the fine folks at the Pragmatic Bookshelf has always been such a great experience that I decided to see if they would work with me again. I'm so grateful to Dave and Andy for letting me work with them again.

Thanks to my awesome editor, Susannah Pfalzer, the book you're reading is in much better shape. Her guidance was essential in keeping things focused, on track, and readable.

The folks that volunteered their time to review this book provided some of the most interesting and thoughtful comments I've seen. Thanks to them, this book has a bunch of wonderful ideas, too. Thanks so much to Jeff Holland, Austen Ott, Kevin Gisi, Tony Collen, Charley Stran, Chris Johnson, Drew Neil, Darcy Laycock, Luke Chadwick, Jeff Carley, Marc Harter, and Nick LaMuro for the great suggestions.

Special thanks to Chris Warren, Mike Weber, Aaron Godin, Emma Smith, Erich Tesky, and the rest of my business associates for their support, and to Chris Johnson for getting me hooked on using tmux in the first place.

Finally, I'm extremely grateful for the continued support of my wife Carissa, who works hard to wrangle our daughters so I can carve out time to write.

Preface

Your mouse is slowing you down.

The mouse, when introduced, created a new way for us to interact with our computers. We could click, double-click, triple-click, and now even swipe to interact with our applications. The mouse, along with graphical interfaces, made computers just a little easier to use for average users. But there's a downside to the mouse, especially for programmers.

As we build software, we work with multiple programs throughout the course of our day. A web developer, for example, might have a database console, web server, and a text editor running at the same time. Switching between these with the mouse eats up valuable time and can break your focus. It may not seem like much, but moving your hand off of the keyboard's home row, placing it on the mouse, locating the pointer, and performing the task can be pretty distracting.

Using tmux, you can create an environment like the one shown in Figure 1, *tmux as a development environment*, on page x. Using tmux's windows, you can easily manage the text editor, the database console, and the local web server within a single environment. And you can split tmux windows into sections, so multiple apps can run side by side. This means you can run a text-based browser, IRC client, or your automated tests in the same window as your main editor.

Best of all, you can quickly move between these windows and panes using only the keyboard, which will greatly increase both your concentration and your productivity.

In this book, you'll learn how to configure, use, and customize tmux. You'll learn how to manage multiple programs simultaneously, write scripts to create custom environments, and find out how to use tmux to work remotely with others. With tmux, you can create a work environment that keeps almost everything you need at your fingertips.

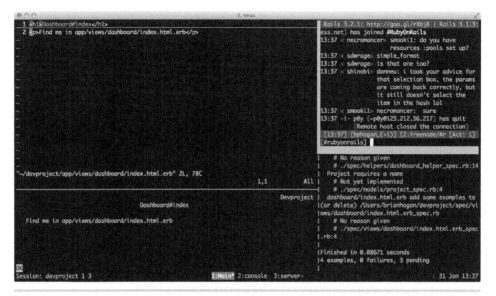

Figure 1—tmux as a development environment

What Is tmux?

tmux is a *terminal multiplexer*. It lets us use a single environment to launch multiple terminals, or windows, each running its own process or program. For example, we can launch tmux and load up the Vim text editor. We can then create a new window, load up a database console, and switch back and forth between these programs all within a single session.

If you use a modern operating system and a terminal that has tabs, this doesn't sound like anything new. But running multiple programs simultaneously is only one of tmux's features. We can divide windows into horizontal or vertical panes, which means we can run two or more programs on the same screen side by side. And we can do it all without using the mouse.

We can also *detach* from a session, meaning we can leave our environment running in the background. If you've used GNU-Screen before, you're familiar with this feature. In many ways, tmux is like GNU-Screen with a lot of extra features, and a much simpler configuration system. And since tmux uses a client-server model, we can control windows and panes from a central location, or even jump between multiple sessions from a single terminal window. This client-server model also lets us create scripts and interact with tmux from other windows or applications.

Over the course of this book, we'll explore all of these features and more.

Who Should Read This Book

This book aims to help application developers who work on OS X or Linux operating systems and spend a good part of their time using the terminal.

If you're a software developer, you'll see how to use tmux to build a development environment that can make working with multiple terminal sessions a breeze. And if you're already comfortable using Vim or Emacs, you'll see how tmux can accelerate your workflow even more.

If you're a system administrator or a developer who spends some time working with remote servers, you'll be interested in how you can leverage tmux to create a persistent dashboard for monitoring servers.

What's In This Book

This book will show you how to incorporate tmux into your work by taking you through its basic features and showing you how you might apply them to everyday situations.

In Chapter 1, *Learning The Basics*, on page 1, you'll learn about the basic features of tmux as you create sessions, panes, and windows and learn how to perform basic navigation.

In Chapter 2, *Configuring tmux*, on page 15, you'll learn how to redefine many of the default keybindings and the appearance of tmux.

In Chapter 3, *Scripting Customized tmux Environments*, on page 33, you'll see how to script your own development environment using the command-line interface, configuration files, and the tmuxinator program.

After that, you'll work with text in Chapter 4, *Working With Text and Buffers*, on page 45. You'll see how to use keyboard keys to move backwards through the buffer, how to select and copy text, and how to work with multiple paste buffers.

Next, in Chapter 5, *Pair Programming with tmux*, on page 53, you'll learn how to set up tmux so that you and a coworker can work together on the same codebasc from dilferent computers using tmux.

Finally, Chapter 6, *Workflows*, on page 59 covers more advanced ways to manage windows, panes, and sessions, and shows you how to be even more productive with tmux.

Changes in This Release

tmux is evolving and this book has a few changes to keep it up to date with the most recent version.

- All examples require at least tmux 1.7, and will work with version 1.8.

- The section on opening panes in the current directory under OS X was removed.

- *Maximizing and Restoring Panes*, on page 60 now states that this behavior is already supported in tmux 1.8.

- The Workflows chapter contains a new section, *Issuing Commands In Many Panes Simultaneously*, on page 62, on using the "synchronize panes" feature.

- All errata have been dealt with, including a couple of nasty typos.

What You Need

In order to use tmux, you'll need a computer that runs Mac OS X or a flavor of UNIX or Linux. Unfortunately, tmux does not run under Windows, but it will run great on a virtual machine, VPS, or shared hosting environment running Linux.

While not required, experience with text editors such as Vim or Emacs will be helpful. tmux works very much the same way, and it has some predefined keyboard shortcuts that users of these editors will find familiar.

Conventions

tmux is a tool that's driven by the keyboard. You'll encounter many keyboard shortcuts throughout the book. Since tmux supports both lower- and upper-case keyboard shortcuts, it may sometimes be unclear which key the book is referencing.

To keep it simple, these are the conventions I've used.

- CTRL-b means "press the CTRL and b keys simultaneously."

- CTRL-R means you'll press the CTRL and r keys simultaneously, but you'll need to use the SHIFT key to produce the capital "R." I won't explicitly show the SHIFT key in any of these keystrokes.

- CTRL-b d means "press the CONTROL and b keys simultaneously, then release, and then press d." In Chapter 1, *Learning The Basics*, on page 1, you'll learn about the *command prefix*, which will use this notation, but shortened to PREFIX d.

- Finally, I'll show some terminal commands throughout the book, like

```
$ tmux new-session
```

The dollar sign is simply the prompt from the shell session and you won't need to type it when you type the command.

Online Resources

The book's web site[1] has links to an interactive discussion forum as well as a place to submit crrata for the book. You'll also find the source code for the configuration files and scripts we build in this book. You can click the box above the code excerpts to download that source code directly.

Working with tmux has made me much more productive, and I'm excited to share my experiences with you. Let's get started by installing tmux and working with its basic features.

---

1.   http://pragprog.com/titles/bhtmux

CHAPTER 1

Learning The Basics

tmux can be an incredible productivity booster once you get the hang of it. In this chapter you'll get acquainted with tmux's basic features as you manage applications within sessions, windows, and panes. These simple concepts make up the foundation of what makes tmux an amazing environment for developers and system administrators alike.

But before you can learn how to use these basic features, you need to get tmux installed.

1.1 Installing tmux

You can install tmux in one of two ways: using a package manager for your operating system, or building tmux from source.

Whichever method you choose, you'll want to ensure you install tmux version 1.7 or higher. Earlier versions of tmux don't support some of the features we're going to cover.

Installing Via a Package Manager

tmux is available in many package managers. On OS X, you can get tmux using Homebrew[1] or Macports.[2] Installation of these package managers is beyond the scope of this book; consult the web page for the manager of your choice. For either one, you'll need Xcode, which you can install through the Mac App Store.

If you use Homebrew, you can install tmux like this:

```
$ brew install tmux
```

1. http://mxcl.github.com/homebrew/
2. http://www.macports.org/

If you use MacPorts, you can install tmux with this command:

```
$ sudo port install tmux
```

On Ubuntu, you can grab tmux with

```
$ sudo apt-get install tmux
```

To ensure that tmux is installed properly, and to check that you have the correct version, execute this command from your terminal:

```
$ tmux -V
tmux 1.8
```

Depending on your package manager, you may not be able to get the most recent version of tmux, which means you'll need to compile and install tmux from source. Let's explore what it takes to do that.

Installing from Source

The process of installing tmux is the same on both Mac OS X and Linux. You'll need the GCC compiler in either case.

For Mac users, that means installing Xcode through the Mac App Store and then installing the Command Line Tools through Xcode by going to Preferences, selecting the Downloads tab, and pressing Install next to the Command Line Tools item.

For Linux users, the package management tools usually have the GCC compilers. On Ubuntu, you simply type

```
$ sudo apt-get install build-essential
```

to get all the compilers you need.

tmux also depends on libevent and ncurses, and you'll need the prerequisites for these as well. On Ubuntu, you can install these using the package manager like this:

```
$ sudo apt-get install libevent-dev libncurses-dev
```

Once you have the compilers and prerequisites installed, grab the tmux source code and download it.[3] Untar the downloaded version and install it like this:

```
$ tar -zxvf tmux-1.8.tar.gz
$ cd tmux-1.8
$ ./configure
$ make
$ sudo make install
```

---

3. http://tmux.sourceforge.net/

You can test out the installation by executing this from the terminal, which returns the currently installed version of tmux:

```
$ tmux -V
tmux 1.8
```

Now that we have tmux properly installed, we can explore the core features of tmux, starting with a basic session.

1.2 Starting tmux

Starting tmux is as easy as typing

```
$ tmux
```

from a terminal window. You'll see something that looks like Figure 2, *New tmux session*, on page 4 appear on your screen. This is a tmux "session," and it works just like your normal terminal session. You can issue any terminal command you'd like and everything will work as expected.

To close the tmux session, simply type

```
$ exit
```

in the session itself. This closes tmux and returns back to the standard terminal.

But, unless you're only using tmux for a very brief period, this isn't the best way to work with sessions in tmux. We can instead create "named sessions" that we can then identify later.

Creating Named Sessions

We can actually have multiple sessions on a single computer, and we'll want to be able to keep them organized. We can do that by giving each session we create its own unique name. Let's create a named session called "basic" right now:

```
$ tmux new-session -s basic
```

We can shorten this command to

```
$ tmux new -s basic
```

which is the convention you'll see throughout the rest of the book.

When we enter this command, we'll be brought into a brand new tmux session, but we won't really notice anything special or different than if we started things up normally. If we typed exit, we'd just be right back at the terminal.

Figure 2—New tmux session

But named sessions come in handy when we want to leave tmux running in the background, which we'll discuss next. But before we continue, type

```
$ exit
```

to exit tmux.

1.3 Detaching and Attaching Sessions

One of tmux's biggest advantages is that we can fire it up, start up programs or processes inside the tmux environment, and then leave it running in the background by "detaching" from the session.

If we close a regular terminal session, all the programs we have running in that session are killed off. But when we detach from a tmux session, we're not actually closing tmux. Any programs we started up in that session will stay running. We can then "attach" to the session and pick up where we left off. To demonstrate, let's create a new named tmux session, start up a program, and detach from the session. First, we create the session:

```
$ tmux new -s basic
```

Then, within the tmux session, we start an application called top, which monitors our memory and CPU usage, like this:

```
$ top
```

We now have something that looks like Figure 3, *The top command running in tmux*, on page 6 running in our terminal. We can now detach from the tmux session by pressing CTRL-b followed by d. This returns us to our regular terminal prompt. We'll learn how to get back into that session shortly, but first, let's talk about the command prefix.

The Command Prefix

Since our programs are running inside tmux, we need a way to tell tmux that the command we're typing is for tmux and not for the underlying application. The CTRL-b combination does just that.

When we wanted to detach from our tmux session, we pressed CTRL-b, followed by d for "detach." We have to prefix each tmux command with this key combination, and it's important to note that we don't hold all these keys down together, but we instead first press CTRL-b simultaneously, release those keys, and then immediately press the key for the command we want to send to tmux.

Throughout the rest of this book, we'll simply use the notation PREFIX, followed by the shortcut key for our commands, like PREFIX d for detaching from a session. In Chapter 2, *Configuring tmux*, on page 15, we'll remap the prefix to an easier combination, but until then, we'll use the defaults.

Now, let's learn how to get back in to that tmux session we left running. But before we do, close your terminal window.

Reattaching to Existing Sessions

We've set up a tmux session, fired up a program inside the session, detached from it, and closed our terminal session, but the tmux session is still chugging along, along with the top application we launched.

We can list existing tmux sessions using the command

```
$ tmux list-sessions
```

in a new terminal window. We can shorten this command to this:

```
$ tmux ls
```

The command shows that we have one session currently running:

```
basic: 1 windows (created Mon Jan 30 16:58:26 2012) [105x25]
```

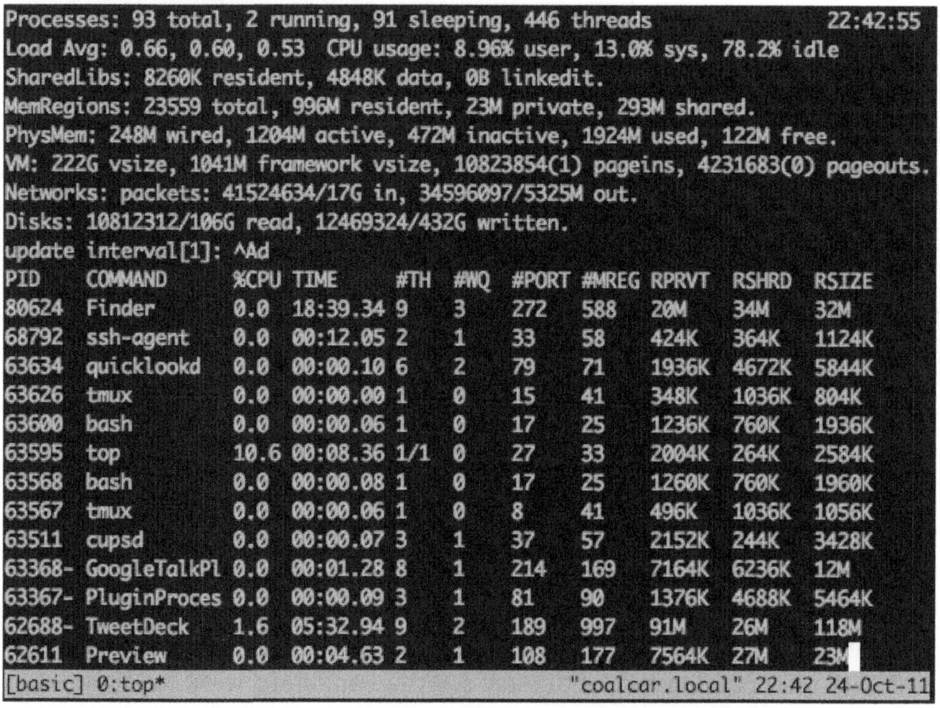

```
Processes: 93 total, 2 running, 91 sleeping, 446 threads          22:42:55
Load Avg: 0.66, 0.60, 0.53  CPU usage: 8.96% user, 13.0% sys, 78.2% idle
SharedLibs: 8260K resident, 4848K data, 0B linkedit.
MemRegions: 23559 total, 996M resident, 23M private, 293M shared.
PhysMem: 248M wired, 1204M active, 472M inactive, 1924M used, 122M free.
VM: 222G vsize, 1041M framework vsize, 10823854(1) pageins, 4231683(0) pageouts.
Networks: packets: 41524634/17G in, 34596097/5325M out.
Disks: 10812312/106G read, 12469324/432G written.
update interval[1]: ^Ad
PID    COMMAND      %CPU TIME      #TH  #WQ  #PORT #MREG RPRVT  RSHRD  RSIZE
80624  Finder       0.0  18:39.34 9    3    272   588   20M    34M    32M
68792  ssh-agent    0.0  00:12.05 2    1    33    58    424K   364K   1124K
63634  quicklookd   0.0  00:00.10 6    2    79    71    1936K  4672K  5844K
63626  tmux         0.0  00:00.00 1    0    15    41    348K   1036K  804K
63600  bash         0.0  00:00.06 1    0    17    25    1236K  760K   1936K
63595  top          10.6 00:08.36 1/1  0    27    33    2004K  264K   2584K
63568  bash         0.0  00:00.08 1    0    17    25    1260K  760K   1960K
63567  tmux         0.0  00:00.06 1    0    8     41    496K   1036K  1056K
63511  cupsd        0.0  00:00.07 3    1    37    57    2152K  244K   3428K
63368- GoogleTalkPl 0.0  00:01.28 8    1    214   169   7164K  6236K  12M
63367- PluginProces 0.0  00:00.09 3    1    81    90    1376K  4688K  5464K
62688- TweetDeck    1.6  05:32.94 9    2    189   997   91M    26M    118M
62611  Preview      0.0  00:04.63 2    1    108   177   7564K  27M    23M
[basic] 0:top*                                    "coalcar.local" 22:42 24-Oct-11
```

Figure 3—The top command running in tmux

To attach to the session, we use the attach keyword. If we only have one session
running, we can simply attach to it with

```
$ tmux attach
```

and we'll be attached to the session again. Things get a little more tricky if
we have more than one session running. Let's detach from the basic session
with PREFIX d.

Now, if we create a new tmux instance in the background using the command

```
$ tmux new -s second_session -d
```

and list the sessions again, we'll see this:

```
$ tmux ls
basic: 1 windows (created Mon Jan 30 16:58:26 2012) [105x25]
second_session: 1 windows (created Mon Jan 30 17:49:21 2012) [105x25]
```

We can attach to the session we want by using the -t flag:

```
$ tmux attach -t second_session
```

This puts us in the second_session tmux session. We can detach from this session just as we did previously, and then attach to a different session. In *Moving Between Sessions*, on page 62 you'll see some other ways to move between active sessions. But for now, let's remove the active sessions.

Killing Sessions

We can type exit within a session to destroy the session, but we can also kill off sessions with the kill-session command.

```
$ tmux kill-session -t basic
$ tmux kill-session -t second_session
```

This is useful for situations where a program in a session is hanging.

If we list the sessions again, we'll get this message:

```
$ tmux ls
failed to connect to server
```

Since there are no tmux sessions running, tmux itself isn't running, so it isn't able to handle the request.

Now that you know the basics of creating and working with sessions, let's look at how we can work with multiple programs within a single session.

1.4 Working with Windows

It's possible, and very common, to run multiple, simultaneous commands within a tmux session. We can keep these organized with windows, which are similar to tabs in modern graphical terminal emulators or web browsers.

When we create a new tmux session, the environment sets up an initial window for us. We can create as many as we'd like, and they will persist when we detach and reattach.

Let's create a new session that has two windows. The first window will have our normal prompt, and the second window will run the top command. We'll create a named session called "windows," like this:

```
$ tmux new -s windows -n shell
```

By using the -n flag, we tell tmux to name the first window so we can identify it easily.

Now let's add a window to this session.

Creating and Naming Windows

To create a window in a current session, we simply press `PREFIX` `c`. Creating a window like this automatically brings the new window into focus. From here, we can start up another application. Let's start `top` in this new window.

```
$ top
```

Our first window has a name we defined, called "shell," but our second window now appears to have the name "top." This window's name changes based on the app that's currently running because we never gave it a default name when we created it. Let's give this window a proper name.

To rename a window, we press `PREFIX` followed by `,` (a comma) and the status bar changes, letting us rename the current window. Go ahead and rename the window to "Processes."

We can create as many windows in a tmux session as we'd like. But once we have more than one, we need to be able to move between them.

Moving Between Windows

We've created two windows in our environment, and we can navigate around our windows in several ways. When we only have two windows, we can quickly move between the windows with `PREFIX` `n`, or "next window." This simply cycles through the windows we have open. Since we only have two windows right now, this just toggles between them.

We can use `PREFIX` `p` to go to the *previous* window.

By default, windows in tmux each have a number, starting at 0. We can quickly jump to the first window with `PREFIX` `0`, and the second window with `PREFIX` `1`. This zero-based array of windows isn't always intuitive, and in Chapter 2, *Configuring tmux*, on page 15, you'll see how we can make the list of windows start at one instead of zero.

If we end up with more than nine windows, we can simply use `PREFIX` `f` to find a window by name (if we named our windows), or `PREFIX` `w` to display a visual menu of our windows so we can select the one we'd like.

From here, we can continue creating new windows and launching programs. When we detach from our session and reattach later, our windows will all be where we left them.

To close a window, we can either type "exit" into the prompt in the window, or we can use `PREFIX` `&`, which gives us a confirmation message in the status bar before killing off the window. If we accept, our previous window comes into focus. To completely close out the tmux session, we have to close all the windows.

Creating windows is great, but we can make tmux even more useful by splitting a window into panes.

1.5 Working with Panes

Having programs in separate windows is fine for stuff we don't mind having out of the way. But with tmux, we can take a single session and divide it into panes.

Let's create a new tmux session called "panes" so we can experiment with how panes work. Exit any existing tmux sessions and create a new one like this:

```
$ tmux new -s panes
```

We can split windows vertically or horizontally. Let's split the window in half vertically first, and then horizontally, giving us one large pane on the left and two smaller panes on the right, just like Figure 4, *A tmux session divided into panes*, on page 10.

In the tmux session, press PREFIX %, and the window will divide down the middle and start up a second session in the new pane. In addition, the focus will move to this new pane. Pressing PREFIX " (double quote) will split this new pane in half horizontally. By default, new panes split the existing pane in half evenly.

To cycle through the panes, press PREFIX o. We can also use PREFIX, followed by the UP, DOWN, LEFT, or RIGHT keys to move around the panes.

With just a couple keystrokes, we've divided one window into a workspace with three panes. Let's look at how we can rearrange these panes with layouts.

Pane Layouts

We can resize a pane, either using incremental resizing or by using templates. Resizing panes incrementally using the default keybindings is quite awkward. In Chapter 2, *Configuring tmux*, on page 15, we'll define some shortcuts to make resizing panes easier. For now, we'll use one of tmux's several default pane layouts:

- even-horizontal stacks all panes horizontally, left to right.
- even-vertical stacks all panes vertically, top to bottom.

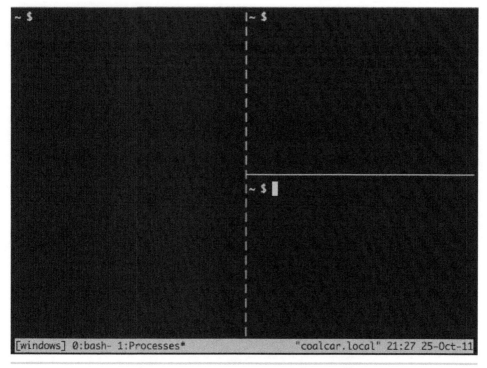

Figure 4—A tmux session divided into panes

- main-horizontal creates one larger pane on the top and smaller panes underneath.

- main-vertical creates one large pane on the left side of the screen, and stacks the rest of the panes vertically on the right.

- tiled arranges all panes evenly on the screen.

We can cycle through these layouts by pressing PREFIX SPACEBAR.

Closing Panes

We can close a pane the same way we exit a terminal session or a tmux window: we simply type "exit" in the pane. You can also kill a pane with PREFIX x, which also closes the window if there's only one pane in that window.

You'll be asked to confirm if you want to kill the specified pane. Killing a pane like this is great for situations where the pane has gotten stuck, or you can't interact with it anymore.

So far, we've been able to create new sessions, create windows and panes, and move around a bit. Before we move on to more advanced topics, let's explore some tmux commands.

1.6 Working with Command Mode

So far, we've used key combinations to create windows and panes, but those keybindings are actually just shortcuts for tmux commands with some preset options. We can execute tmux commands two ways: from the terminal itself or from the "command area" in the tmux status bar. You'll learn about using tmux commands from the terminal in Chapter 3, *Scripting Customized tmux Environments*, on page 33, but for now, let's explore tmux's Command mode by using it to create some new windows and panes in our workspace.

To enter Command mode, press PREFIX : (the colon) from within a running tmux session. The status bar changes color and we get a command prompt that indicates that we can type our command. Let's create a new window by using the new-window command, like this:

```
new-window -n console
```

By using a command rather than the shortcut, we were able to create a new window and give it a name at the same time, by using the -n flag. Let's take this a step further and launch a new window that starts the top program. To do that, we enter Command mode and type this command:

```
new-window -n processes "top"
```

When we press ENTER, our new window appears and we see the top application running, showing our running processes.

Specifying an initial command for a window is extremely handy for short-term tasks, but if we exit the top app by pressing q, the tmux window we created will also close. You can use configuration settings to get around this, but if you want the window to persist, simply create it without specifying an initial command, and then execute your own command in the new window.

We can use Command mode to create new windows, new panes, or new sessions, or even set other environmental options. In Chapter 2, *Configuring tmux*, on page 15, we'll create a few custom keybindings to make some of these commands easier to use.

1.7 What's Next?

In this chapter, we covered the very basic usage of tmux sessions, panes, windows, and commands, but there's a lot more we can explore.

By pressing `PREFIX` `?`, you can get a list of all predefined tmux keybindings and the associated commands these trigger.

As you work with tmux, think about how you can create different environments for your work. If you're monitoring servers, you could use tmux panes to create a dashboard that shows your various monitoring scripts and log files.

With the basics under our belt, let's put together a custom configuration we can use for the rest of our work.

For Future Reference

Creating Sessions

Command	Description
tmux new-session	Creates a new session without a name. Can be shortened to tmux new or simply tmux.
tmux new -s development	Creates a new session called "development."
tmux new -s development -n editor	Creates a session named "development" and names the first window "editor."
tmux attach -t development	Attaches to a session named "development."

Default Commands for Sessions, Windows, and Panes

Command	Description
`PREFIX` `d`	Detaches from the session, leaving the session running in the background.
`PREFIX` `:`	Enters Command mode.
`PREFIX` `c`	Creates a new window from within an existing tmux session. Shortcut for new-window.
`PREFIX` `0`...`9`	Selects windows by number.
`PREFIX` `w`	Displays a selectable list of windows in the current session.
`PREFIX` `,`	Displays a prompt to rename a window.
`PREFIX` `&`	Closes the current window after prompting for confirmation.

Command	Description
`PREFIX` `%`	Divides the current window in half vertically.
`PREFIX` `"`	Divides the current window in half horizontally.
`PREFIX` `o`	Cycles through open panes.
`PREFIX` `q`	Momentarily displays pane numbers in each pane.
`PREFIX` `x`	Closes the current pane after prompting for confirmation.
`PREFIX` `SPACE`	Cycles through the various pane layouts.

## CHAPTER 2

Configuring tmux

tmux, by default, doesn't have the most friendly commands. Many of the most important and useful features are assigned to hard-to-reach keystrokes or consist of long, verbose command strings. And tmux's default color scheme isn't very easy on the eyes. In this chapter, we're going to build a basic configuration file for our tmux installation that we'll then use for the rest of this book. We'll start out by customizing how we navigate around the screen and how we create and resize panes, and then we'll discuss how we can tackle some more advanced settings. We'll also make sure your Terminal is properly configured so that some of the settings we make to tmux's appearance look good on your screen. When we're done, you'll have a better understanding of how flexible tmux is, and you can start making it your own. Let's start by talking about how we actually configure tmux in the first place.

2.1 Introducing the .tmux.conf File

By default, tmux looks for configuration settings in two places. It first looks in /etc/tmux.conf for a system-wide configuration. It then looks for a file called .tmux.conf in the current user's home directory. If these files don't exist, tmux simply uses its default settings. We don't need to create a system-wide configuration, so let's create a brand new configuration file in our home directory.

```
$ touch ~/.tmux.conf
```

In this file we can do everything from defining new key shortcuts to setting up a default environment with multiple windows, panes, and running programs. Let's start by setting a couple basic options that will make working with tmux much easier.

Remapping the Caps Lock Key

On many keyboards, the CAPS LOCK key sits right next to the a key on the home row of the keyboard. By remapping this key to CTRL, you can make triggering commands more comfortable.

On OS X, you can remap the CAPS LOCK key under the Keyboard preference pane, under System Preferences. Just press the Modifier Keys button and change the action for CAPS LOCK to "Control."

Under Linux, the process can be a little more tricky depending on your distribution or window manager, but you can find several methods described on the Emacs wiki.[a]

This small change to your configuration can save you a surprising amount of time over the course of a day.

_____

a.   http://www.emacswiki.org/emacs/MovingTheCtrlKey

Defining an Easier Prefix

As you saw earlier, tmux uses CTRL-b as its command prefix. Many tmux users started out using GNU-Screen, which uses CTRL-a for its command prefix. CTRL-a is an excellent choice for a prefix because it's easier to trigger, especially if you've remapped your computer's CAPS LOCK key to CTRL as explained in *Remapping the Caps Lock Key*, on page 16. This keeps your hands on the home row of your keyboard.

To set options in the .tmux.conf file, we use the set-option command, which we can shorten to set. Let's redefine our tmux prefix by adding this code to our .tmux.conf file:

```
config/tmux.conf
set -g prefix C-a
```

In this example, we're using the -g switch, for "global," which sets the option for all tmux sessions we create.

While not necessary, we can use the unbind-key, or unbind command to remove a keybinding that's been defined, so we can assign a different command to this key later. Let's free up CTRL-b like this:

```
unbind C-b
```

Changes to the file aren't read by tmux automatically. So if you're editing your .tmux.conf file while tmux is running you'll either need to completely close *all* tmux sessions, or enter tmux's Command mode with PREFIX : and type this whenever you make a change:

```
source-file ~/.tmux.conf
```

We can now use CTRL-a for our prefix. We'll still continue to refer to it as PREFIX in the rest of the examples in the book.

Changing the Default Delay

tmux adds a very small delay when sending commands, and this delay can interfere with other programs such as the Vim text editor. We can set this delay so it's much more responsive:

```
set -s escape-time 1
```

Once we reload our configuration file, we can issue keystrokes without delay.

Setting the Window and Panes Index

In Chapter 1, *Learning The Basics*, on page 1, we discussed windows, and how when we create more than one window in a session, we reference windows by their index. This index starts at zero, which can be a little awkward. By adding this line to our configuration file:

```
set -g base-index 1
```

the window index will start at 1. This also means we can use PREFIX 1 to jump to the first window, instead of PREFIX 0.

We can also set the starting index for panes using the pane-base-index option. Let's add this line to our configuration so we have some consistency between our pane and window numbering.

```
setw -g pane-base-index 1
```

Up until now, we've used the set command, which sets options for the tmux session. In order to configure options that affect how we interact with windows, we have to use another command, called set-window-option, which we can shorten to setw. In this book, I've used the shortened versions of commands to make the configuration examples fit on one line, but you'll need to pay special attention, because set and setw are easy to mix up.

Now let's build some useful shortcuts that will increase our productivity.

2.2 Customizing Keys, Commands, and User Input

Many of the default keyboard shortcuts in tmux are a bit of a stretch, both physically and mentally. Not only is PREFIX % hard to press, as it involves holding three keys, but without looking at the command reference, there's no easy way to remember what it does.

In this section, we'll define, or redefine, some of the most-used tmux commands. Let's start by creating a custom keybinding to reload our tmux configuration.

Creating a Shortcut to Reload the Configuration

Every time we make a change to our configuration file, we either have to shut down *all* sessions and then restart tmux, or issue a command to reload our configuration from within the running instances. Let's create a custom keybinding to reload the configuration file.

We use the bind command to define a new keybinding. We specify the key we want to use, followed by the command we want to perform.

For our first keybinding, we'll set PREFIX r so it reloads our main .tmux.conf file in the current session.

```
bind r source-file ~/.tmux.conf
```

When we define keybindings using bind, we still have to push the PREFIX key before we can press the newly defined key. And while we just defined a new command to make reloading the tmux configuration easier, we can't use it until we reload the configuration file. So be sure to enter Command mode with PREFIX : and type

```
source-file ~/.tmux.conf
```

one more time.

When we reload the file, we won't always be able to tell that anything changed, but we can use the display command to put a message in the status line. Let's modify our reload command to display "Reloaded!" when the configuration file loads:

config/tmux.conf
```
bind r source-file ~/.tmux.conf \; display "Reloaded!"
```

We can bind a key to a series of commands by separating the commands with the \; character combination.

With this keybinding in place, we can make additional changes to the configuration file and then immediately activate them by pressing PREFIX r.

> \\//   **Joe asks:**
> ⁶ȳ̆   **Can I Define Keybindings That Don't Require a Prefix?**
>
> Absolutely. Using the bind command with the -n prefix tells tmux that the keybinding doesn't require pressing the prefix. For example,
>
> **bind-key** -n C-r **source-file** ~/.tmux.conf
>
> would make CTRL-r reload the configuration file. Unfortunately this would completely disable that key combination in any application that's running in a tmux session, so you'll want to use this with care.

Sending the Prefix to Other Applications

We've remapped CTRL-a as our Prefix, but programs such as Vim, Emacs, and even the regular Bash shell also use that combination. We need to configure tmux to let us send that command through when we need it. We can do that by binding the send-prefix command to a keystroke, like this:

```
bind C-a send-prefix
```

After reloading the configuration file, we can send CTRL-a to an application running within tmux simply by pressing CTRL-a twice.

Splitting Panes

The default keys for splitting panes can be difficult to remember, so let's set our own keys that we won't be able to forget. We'll set the horizontal split to PREFIX | and the vertical split to PREFIX -.

```
bind | split-window -h
bind - split-window -v
```

At first glance, this may look backwards. The -v and -h flags on split-window stand for "vertical" and "horizontal" splits, but to tmux, a vertical split means creating a new pane below the existing pane so the panes are stacked vertically on top of each other. A horizontal split means creating a new pane *next* to the existing one so the panes are stacked horizontally across the screen. So, in order to divide the window vertically, we use a "horizontal" split, and to divide it horizontally, we use a "vertical" split.

These new shortcuts give us a nice visual association. If we want our windows split, we simply press the key that looks like the split we want to create.

Remapping Movement Keys

Moving from pane to pane with PREFIX o is a little cumbersome, and using the arrow keys means we have to take our fingers off the home row. If you use the Vim text editor, you're probably familiar with its use of h, j, k, and l for movement keys. We can remap the movement keys in tmux to these same keys.

```
config/tmux.conf
bind h select-pane -L
bind j select-pane -D
bind k select-pane -U
bind l select-pane -R
```

In addition, we can use PREFIX CTRL-h and PREFIX CTRL-l to cycle through the windows by binding those keystrokes to the respective commands:

```
bind -r C-h select-window -t :-
bind -r C-l select-window -t :+
```

Provided you've mapped your CAPS LOCK key to the CTRL key, you can now move between panes without moving your hands off the home row.

Resizing Panes

To resize a pane, we can enter Command mode and type resize-pane -D to resize a pane downward one row at a time. We can increase the resizing increment by passing a number after the direction, such as resize-pane -D 5, but the command itself is pretty verbose. Let's make some keybindings to make resizing panes easier.

Let's use a variation of the Vim movement keys to resize windows. We'll use PREFIX H, PREFIX J, PREFIX K, and PREFIX L to change the size of the panes:

```
bind H resize-pane -L 5
bind J resize-pane -D 5
bind K resize-pane -U 5
bind L resize-pane -R 5
```

Notice that we're using uppercase letters in the configuration file. tmux allows both lowercase and uppercase letters for keystrokes. You'll need to use the SHIFT key to trigger the uppercase keystroke.

Using these movement keys will help us keep track of which way we want the window size to change. For example, if we have a window divided into two panes stacked horizontally, like this:

and we want to increase the size of Pane 1, then we'd place our cursor inside Pane 1 and then press PREFIX J, which will move the horizontal divider *downward*. If we pressed PREFIX K, we would move the horizontal divider up.

We resize panes in increments, so that means that each time we want to resize the pane, we need to use the prefix. But if we use the -r flag, we can specify that we want the key to be *repeatable*, meaning we can press the prefix key only once and then continuously press the defined key within the repeat limit.

```
bind -r H resize-pane -L 5
bind -r J resize-pane -D 5
bind -r K resize-pane -U 5
bind -r L resize-pane -R 5
```

The default repeat limit is 500 milliseconds, and we can change that by setting the repeat-time option to a higher value.

Now let's turn our attention to how tmux can work with the mouse.

Handling the Mouse

While tmux is meant to be completely keyboard-driven, there are times when you may find it easier to use the mouse. If your Terminal is set up to forward mouse clicks and movement through to programs in the terminal, then you can tell tmux how to handle certain mouse events.

Sometimes it's nice to be able to scroll up through the Terminal buffer with the mouse wheel, or to select windows and panes, especially when you're just getting started with tmux. To configure tmux so we can use the mouse, we need to enable mouse mode.

```
setw -g mode-mouse on
```

We could also configure tmux so it will let us use the mouse to select a pane, resize a pane, or even let us click on the window list to select a window. We would do that by setting the corresponding options, like this:

```
set -g mouse-select-pane on
set -g mouse-resize-pane on
set -g mouse-select-window on
```

These can be handy additions to your configuration, but remember that using the mouse with tmux will slow you down. Even though being able to scroll and click might seem like a neat idea, you should learn the keyboard equivalents for switching panes and moving forward and backward through the buffers. So, for our configuration file, we're going to disable all the mouse options. We can do that explicitly like this:

```
setw -g mode-mouse off
set -g mouse-select-pane off
set -g mouse-resize-pane off
set -g mouse-select-window off
```

or by simply disabling the mouse entirely:

```
config/tmux.conf
setw -g mode-mouse off
```

Setting this option prevents us from accidentally doing things when we select the Terminal window with our mouse, and it forces us to get more comfortable with the keyboard.

The flexible configuration system tmux provides lets us completely customize the way we interact with the interface, but we can also configure its appearance to make its interface easier to see, and in some cases, more informative.

2.3 Visual Styling

tmux gives us quite a few ways to customize our environment's appearance. In this section, we'll walk through configuring some of these options, as we customize the status line and other components. We'll start by configuring the colors for various elements, then we'll turn our bland status bar into something that will provide us with some vital information about our environment.

Configuring Colors

To get the best visual experience out of tmux, we have to make sure that both our Terminal and tmux are configured for 256 colors. Let's start by configuring our Terminal first.

We can use a simple Perl script[1] to test the color modes in our Terminal.

---

1.   http://www.vim.org/scripts/script.php?script_id=1349

Figure 5—The Terminal properly displaying 256 colors

```
$ wget http://www.vim.org/scripts/download_script.php?src_id=4568 \
-O colortest
```

```
$ perl colortest -w
```

You should see something like Figure 5, *The Terminal properly displaying 256 colors*, on page 23 in your Terminal if you're configured properly.

If you're using Linux, you might need to add

```
[ -z "$TMUX" ] && export TERM=xterm-256color
```

to your .bashrc file to enable a 256-color Terminal. This conditional statement ensures that the TERM variable is only set outside of tmux, since tmux sets its own terminal.

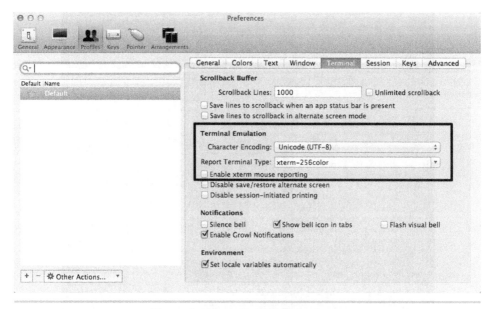

Figure 6—iTerm 2 settings for tmux

If you're using a Mac, you should know that the Terminal app in Snow Leopard only displays 16 colors. You'll need to install an alternative terminal such as iTerm2[2] to get full color support.

If you don't see the correct number of colors, configure your Terminal to use xterm's 256 mode. In iTerm2, you can find this by editing the default profile and changing the Terminal mode to xterm-256color as shown in Figure 6, *iTerm 2 settings for tmux*, on page 24.

Also, ensure that your Terminal emulator supports displaying UTF-8 characters so that visual elements such as the pane dividers appear as dashed lines.

In order to make tmux display things in 256 colors, we add this line to our .tmux.conf file:

config/tmux.conf
```
set -g default-terminal "screen-256color"
```

Once the right color mode is set, you'll find it much easier to use programs such as Vim from within tmux, especially when you are using more complex color schemes for syntax highlighting. Just take a look at Figure 7, *16 colors vs. 256 Colors in Vim*, on page 25 to see the difference. Now let's configure the appearance of tmux's components, starting with colors.

---

2.   http://www.iterm2.com

```
 1 # A simple hello program with tests in Ruby       1 # A simple hello program with tests in Ruby
 2 require 'test/unit'                                2 require 'test/unit'
 3                                                    3
 4 def hello(name)                                    4 def hello(name)
 5   "Hello #{name}"                                  5   "Hello #{name}"
 6 end                                                6 end
 7                                                    7
 8 class HelloTest < Test::Unit::TestCase             8 class HelloTest < Test::Unit::TestCase
 9   def test_hello_uses_name                         9   def test_hello_uses_name
10     assert_equal "Hello Ted", hello("Ted")        10     assert_equal "Hello Ted", hello("Ted")
11   end                                             11   end
12 end                                               12 end
```

Figure 7—16 colors vs. 256 Colors in Vim

Changing Colors

We can change the colors of several parts of the tmux interface, including the status bar, window list, command area, and even the pane dividers.

tmux provides variables we can use to specify colors, including black, red, green, yellow, blue, magenta, cyan, or white. We can use colour0 to colour255 on the 256 color palette. If you look at the output of the colortest program, you can see the color codes available to you. You can also run this simple shell script to get the color variable you'd like to use:[3]

```
for i in {0..255} ; do
  printf "\x1b[38;5;${i}mcolour${i}\n"
done
```

tmux has specific configuration options to change foreground and background colors for each of its components. Let's start exploring these by customizing the colors of our status bar.

Changing the Status Bar Colors

The default status bar has black text on a bright green background. It's pretty bland. Let's make it have white text on a black background by default.

We use the status-bg and status-fg options to set the foreground and background colors of the status bar, so our settings would be like this:

```
set -g status-fg white
set -g status-bg black
```

Later we'll customize the colors of the items within the sidebar. Right now let's customize the window list.

---

3.   http://superuser.com/questions/285381/how-does-the-tmux-color-palette-work

Changing the Window List Colors

We want to make it more apparent which window is active, so we'll style the active window red and the inactive windows cyan. To style the regular windows, we use set-window-option, like this:

```
config/tmux.conf
setw -g window-status-fg cyan
setw -g window-status-bg default
setw -g window-status-attr dim
```

We can use default for a value so it inherits from the color of the status bar. To style the active window, we use a similar set of options:

```
setw -g window-status-current-fg white
setw -g window-status-current-bg red
setw -g window-status-current-attr bright
```

This takes care of the window list, but we can also customize the colors of the pane dividers.

Changing Pane Divider Colors

We can color the pane dividers, which is nice, but we can also define colors to make the active pane more apparent, as in Figure 8, *The active pane*, on page 27.

Panes have both foreground and background colors, so we need to set the variables accordingly:

```
set -g pane-border-fg color
set -g pane-border-bg color

set -g pane-active-border-fg color
set -g pane-active-border-bg color
```

The foreground color of a pane is the actual dashed line that makes up the border. The background color, by default, is black, but if we color it in when the pane is active, we can make the active pane extremely noticeable.

```
set -g pane-border-fg green
set -g pane-border-bg black
set -g pane-active-border-fg white
set -g pane-active-border-bg yellow
```

Before we move on to the status bar, let's touch up the tmux command line.

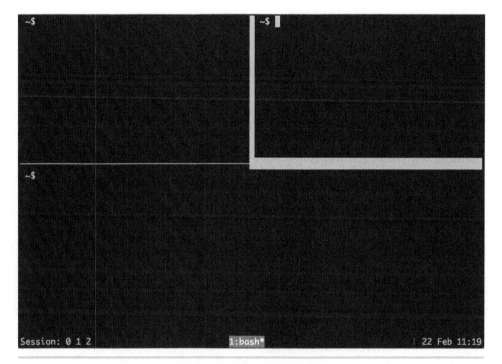

Figure 8—The active pane

Customizing the Command Line

We can also customize the command line, where we enter tmux commands and see alert messages. The approach is almost identical to the way we styled the status line itself.

Let's change the background color to black and the text color to white. We'll use a bright white so the message stands out in more detail.

```
set -g message-fg white
set -g message-bg black
set -g message-attr bright
```

That was easy. Now let's change the areas of the status bar on both sides of the window list.

2.4 Customizing the Status Bar

The tmux status bar can display pretty much any information we want. We can use some predefined components or create our own by executing shell commands.

The status bar, by default, looks like this:

```
[development] 0:bash*                        "example.local" 00:44 02-Nov-1
```

On the left side, we have the name of the tmux session followed by the list of windows. The list of windows shows the numerical index of the current window and its name. On the right side, we have the hostname of our server followed by the date and time. Let's customize the content of our status bar.

Configuring Status Bar Items

The status bar consists of three components: a left panel, the window list, and a right panel. We can change the content in the left or right panels of the status bar using a combination of text and variables. Table 1, *Status line variables*, on page 28 shows the possible variables we can use in our status bar.

Variable	Description
#H	Hostname of local host
#h	Hostname of local host without the domain name
#F	Current window flag
#I	Current window index
#P	Current pane index
#S	Current session name
#T	Current window title
#W	Current window name
##	A literal #
#(shell-command)	First line of the shell command's output
#[attributes]	Color or attribute change

Table 1—Status line variables

For example, if we wanted to show just the name of the current tmux session on the left side, we'd use the set-option -g status-left option with the #S value, like this:

```
set -g status-left "#S"
```

But we can also make it stand out more by using an attribute to set the foreground color, like this:

```
set -g status-left "#[fg=green]#S"
```

We can add as many attributes and items to the status bar as we want. To demonstrate, let's alter the left side of the status bar so it shows the session name in green, the current window number in yellow, and the current pane in cyan.

```
set -g status-left "#[fg=green]#S #[fg=yellow]#I #[fg-cyan]#P"
```

We can add any arbitrary text into the status bar, too. Let's add text to make the session, window, and pane more noticeable, like this:

config/tmux.conf
```
set -g status-left-length 40
set -g status-left "#[fg=green]Session: #S #[fg=yellow]#I #[fg=cyan]#P"
```

We set the status-left-length option because the output we've specified is too long for the default length, so we have to make that region wider.

We can also configure the right side of the status bar. Let's add the current date and time.

```
set -g status-right "#[fg=cyan]%d %b %R"
```

This formats the date as "13-Jan 13:45," but you can format it however you'd like, using the standard strftime() time formatting mechanism used in many programming languages.[4]

It's a good idea to turn on UTF-8 support in the status bar, especially if you're interested in using those characters.

```
set -g status-utf8 on
```

We can take things a step further by incorporating shell commands into the mix by using the #(shell-command) variable to return the result of any external command-line program into the status bar. We'll go into this in detail in *Adding Battery Life to the Status Line*, on page 66.

Keeping Status Bar Info Up to Date

We've added the current time and some other dynamic information to our status bar, but we need to tell tmux how often to refresh that information periodically. By default, tmux refreshes the status bar every 15 seconds. We can specify exactly how quickly tmux refreshes its status bar with set-option -g status-interval followed by the refresh interval in seconds, like this:

```
set -g status-interval 60
```

---

4. See http://www.foragoodstrftime.com/ for a handy tool to help you find the perfect time format.

This would refresh the status bar every 60 seconds. Keep in mind that if you're firing off shell commands, those will be executed once per interval, so be careful not to load too many resource-intensive scripts.

Centering the Window List

We can also control the placement of the window list. By default, the window list is left-aligned, but we can center the window list in between the left and right status areas with a single configuration change:

```
config/tmux.conf
set -g status-justify centre
```

With this in place, the window list appears centered. As we create new windows, the window list shifts accordingly, staying in the center of the status bar.

Identifying Activity in Other Windows

In the same way, we want to be notified when something happens in one of the other windows in our session so we can react to it. We'll do that by adding a visual notification, like this:

```
setw -g monitor-activity on
set -g visual-activity on
```

Now when one of the other windows has some activity, it'll stand out with a cyan background, like the "webserver" window shown here:

```
Session: development 1 1      1:editor* 2:webserver# 3:dbconsole-      30 Jan 21:48
```

2.5 What's Next?

We've built up a pretty solid configuration file throughout this chapter. Look at Appendix 1, *Our Configuration*, on page 69 to see the whole .tmux.conf file.

We can define many additional options in our .tmux.conf file. For example, in Chapter 3, *Scripting Customized tmux Environments*, on page 33, we'll discuss how to set up a custom default work environment using project-specific configuration files.

In addition, you can configure a default configuration for your system in /etc/tmux.conf. This is great for situations where you've set up a shared server so members of your team can collaborate, or if you just want to ensure that every user on the system has some sensible defaults.

Now that we have a configuration defined, let's look at how we can create our own custom development environments with scripts so we can more easily take advantage of these panes and windows without having to set them up each time we start our day.

For Future Reference

Command	Description
set -g prefix C-a	Sets the key combination for the Prefix key.
set -sg escape-time n	Sets the amount of time (in milliseconds) tmux waits for a keystroke after pressing PREFIX.
source-file [file]	Loads a configuration file. Use this to reload the existing configuration or bring in additional configuration options later.
bind C-a send-prefix	Configures tmux to send the prefix when pressing the PREFIX combination twice consecutively.
bind-key [key] [command]	Creates a keybinding that executes the specified command. Can be shortened to bind
bind-key -r [key] [command]	Creates a keybinding that is repeatable, meaning you only need to press the PREFIX key once, and you can press the assigned key repeatedly afterwards. This is useful for commands where you want to cycle through elements or resize panes. Can be shortened to bind.
unbind-key [key]	Removes a defined keybinding so it can be bound to a different command. Can be shortened to unbind.
display-message or display	Displays the given text in the status message.
set-option [flags] [option] [value]	Sets options for sessions. Using the -g flag sets the option for all sessions.
set-window-option [option] [value]	Sets options for windows, such as activity notifications, cursor movement, or other elements related to windows and panes.
set -a	Appends values onto existing options rather than replacing the option's value.

## CHAPTER 3

Scripting Customized tmux Environments

You probably run a wide collection of tools and programs as you work on your projects. If you're working on a web application, you most likely need to have a command shell, a text editor, a database console, and another window dedicated to running your automated test suite for your application. That's a lot of windows to manage, and a lot of commands to type to get it all fired up.

Imagine being able to come to your workstation, ready to tackle that new feature, and being able to bring every one of those programs up, each in its own pane or window in a single tmux session, using a single command. We can use tmux's client-server model to create custom scripts that build up our development environments, splitting windows and launching programs for us automatically. We'll explore how to do this manually first, and then we'll look at more advanced automatic tools.

3.1 Creating a Custom Setup with tmux Commands

We've already explored how we use the tmux command to create new tmux sessions, but the tmux command takes many other options. We can take an existing session and split its windows into panes, change layouts, or even start up applications within the session.

The key to this is the -t switch, or the "target." When we have a named tmux session, we can attach to it like this:

```
$ tmux attach -t [session_name]
```

We use this target switch to direct the command to the appropriate tmux session. So, if we create a new tmux session called "development," like this:

```
$ tmux new-session -s development
```

and we then detach from the session with PREFIX d, then we could split that window horizontally by issuing this command:

```
$ tmux split-window -h -t development
```

When we attach to the window again, we'll have our window split into two panes.

```
$ tmux attach -t development
```

In fact, we don't even have to detach from a tmux session to send commands. We can open another terminal and split the window again, but this time with a vertical split:

```
$ tmux split-window -v -t development
```

Using this approach, we can customize existing environments easily. Let's explore the various commands by creating our own development environment.

Scripting a Project Configuration

In Chapter 1, *Learning The Basics*, on page 1, we discussed tmux commands such as new-session and new-window. Let's write a simple script using these and similar commands that creates a new tmux session and creates a window with a couple panes and two additional windows with one pane each. To top it off, we'll launch applications in each of the panes.

Let's start by creating a new script called development in our home directory. We'll make this script executable too, so we can run it like a regular command.

```
$ touch ~/development
$ chmod +x ~/development
```

Inside this new file, we'll first create a new tmux session called "development."

scripting/development
```
tmux new-session -s development -n editor -d
```

We're passing a couple additional parameters when we create this new session. First, we're creating this session and naming it with the -s flag like we've done before. Then we're giving the initial window a name of "editor," and immediately detaching from this new session with the -d flag.

When we start up our session, we want to change to the directory for our project. We'll call that devproject. And before we can change to that folder, we'd better create it first.

```
$ mkdir ~/devproject
```

With the folder created, we add a line to our configuration that uses tmux's send-keys command to change the directory.

```
tmux send-keys -t development 'cd ~/devproject' C-m
```

We place C-m at the end of the line to send the Carriage Return sequence, represented by Control-M.[1] We can then repeat this command to open the Vim text editor in that window, like this:

```
tmux send-keys -t development 'vim' C-m
```

With these three commands, we've created a new session, changed to a directory, and opened a text editor, but our environment isn't yet complete. Let's split the main editor window so we have a small terminal window on the bottom. We do this with the split-window command. In our script, add this line:

```
tmux split-window -v -t development
```

This splits the main window in half horizontally. We could have specified a percentage using something like

```
tmux split-window -v -p 10 -t development
```

but instead, we'll just leave the split-window command as is and then select one of the default tmux layouts—the main-horizontal one—by adding this to our configuration:

```
tmux select-layout -t development main-horizontal
```

We've created our first window and split it into two panes, but the bottom pane needs to open in the project folder. We already know how we send commands to tmux instances, but now we have to target those commands at specific panes and windows.

Targeting Specific Panes and Windows

With commands such as send-keys, we can specify not only the target session, but also the target window and pane. In our configuration file back in Chapter 2, *Configuring tmux*, on page 15, we specified a base-index of 1, meaning that our window numbering starts at 1. This base index doesn't affect the panes, though, which is why we also set the pane-base-index to 1. In our case, we have two panes in our current setup, as in Figure 9, *Two panes*, on page 36

We have the Vim text editor open in Pane 1, and we want to send a command to Pane 2 that changes to our project directory. We target a pane using the

___
1. http://en.wikipedia.org/wiki/Carriage_return

Figure 9—Two panes

format [session]:[window].[pane]—in our case, development:1.2. So, we add this line to our configuration script, and we get exactly what we want.

```
tmux send-keys -t development:1.2 'cd ~/devproject' C-m
```

We're almost there. We can use what we've learned to finish up our configuration by adding a couple additional windows to the session.

Creating and Selecting Windows

We want a second window in our session that will be a full-screen console. We can create that new window using the new-window command.

```
tmux new-window -n console -t development
tmux send-keys -t development:2 'cd ~/devproject' C-m
```

After we create the window, we use send-keys to once again change into our project directory. We only have one pane in our new window, so we only have to specify the window number in the target.

When we start up our session, we want our first window to be displayed, and we do that with the select-window command:

```
tmux select-window -t development:1
tmux attach -t development
```

We could continue to add to this script, creating additional windows and panes, starting up remote connections to our servers, tailing log files, connecting to database consoles, or even running commands that pull down the latest version of our code when we start working. But we'll stop here, and simply end our script by finally attaching to the session so it shows up on the screen, ready for us to begin working. Our entire script looks like this:

```
tmux new-session -s development -n editor -d
tmux send-keys -t development 'cd ~/devproject' C-m
tmux send-keys -t development 'vim' C-m
tmux split-window -v -t development
tmux select-layout -t development main-horizontal
tmux send-keys -t development:1.2 'cd ~/devproject' C-m
```

```
tmux new-window -n console -t development
tmux send-keys -t development:2 'cd ~/devproject' C-m
tmux select-window -t development:1
tmux attach -t development
```

and when we run it with

$ ~/development

we see an environment that looks like Figure 10, *Our scripted development environment*, on page 38.

One drawback to this approach is that this script creates a brand new session. It won't work properly if you run it a second time while the development session is currently running. You could modify the script to check if a session with that name already exists by using the tmux has-session command and only create the session if it's not there, like this:

scripting/reattach/development
```
tmux has-session -t development
if [ $? != 0 ]
then
  tmux new-session -s development -n editor -d
  tmux send-keys -t development 'cd ~/devproject' C-m
  tmux send-keys -t development 'vim' C-m
  tmux split-window -v -t development
  tmux select-layout -t development main-horizontal
  tmux send-keys -t development:1.2 'cd ~/devproject' C-m
  tmux new-window -n console -t development
  tmux send-keys -t development:2 'cd ~/devproject' C-m
  tmux select-window -t development:1
fi
tmux attach -t development
```

This approach works well for a single project setup. You could modify this further by using a variable for the project name to make the script more generic, but let's look at a couple other ways we can configure things to manage multiple projects.

3.2 Using tmux Configuration for Setup

The .tmux.conf file itself can include commands that set up a default environment. If we wanted every tmux session to start in the same default folder, or automatically open a split window, we could bake that right in to our default configuration, simply by using the appropriate commands.

But we can also specify a configuration file when we start up an instance of tmux, by using the -f flag. This way we don't have to change our original

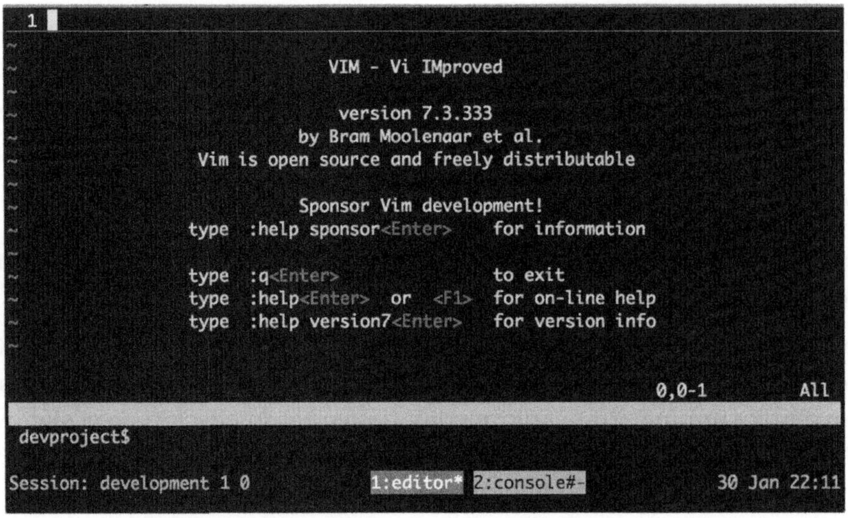

Figure 10—Our scripted development environment

default configuration file, and we can check our configuration file in with our project. We can also set up our own per-project configuration options, such as new keyboard shortcuts.

Let's try this out by creating a file called app.conf. Inside this file, we can use the same commands we learned about in the previous section, but since we're inside the configuration file rather than a shell script, we don't have to explicitly prefix each command with tmux.

scripting/app.conf
```
source-file ~/.tmux.conf
new-session -s development -n editor -d
send-keys -t development 'cd ~/devproject' C-m
send-keys -t development 'vim' C-m
split-window -v -t development
select-layout -t development main-horizontal
send-keys -t development:1.1 'cd ~/devproject' C-m
new-window -n console -t development
send-keys -t development:2 'cd ~/devproject' C-m
select-window -t development:1
```

Notice that we're including our original .tmux.conf file on the first line. This way we'll have all our environment settings we previously defined, including our keybindings and status bar settings. This isn't mandatory, but if we left this off we'd have to use all the default keybindings and options, or we'd have to define our own options in this file.

To use this configuration file, we pass the -f flag followed by the path to the config file. We also have to start tmux with the attach command, like this:

```
$ tmux -f app.conf attach
```

This is because, by default, tmux always calls the new-session command when it starts. Our file creates a new session already, so we'd have *two* tmux sessions running if we left off attach.

This approach gives us a lot of flexibility, but we can gain even more by using a command-line tool called tmuxinator.

3.3   Managing Configuration with tmuxinator

tmuxinator is a simple tool we can use to write and manage different tmux configurations. We define our window layouts and commands in a simple YAML format, and then launch them with the tmuxinator command. Unlike the other approaches, tmuxinator offers a central location for our configurations and a much easier dialect for creating complex layouts. It also lets us specify commands that should always run before each window gets created.

tmuxinator requires the Ruby interpreter, so you'll need to have that on your system. Mac OS X users already have Ruby installed, and Linux users can usually install Ruby through a package manager. However, if you plan to use Ruby for anything beyond tmuxinator, I strongly encourage you to install Ruby through RVM by following along with the instructions on the RVM web site.[2]

We install tmuxinator using Rubygems, the package management system for Ruby.

```
$ gem install tmuxinator
```

If you're not using RVM, you'll need to run this as root or with the sudo command.

tmuxinator needs the $EDITOR shell environment to be defined, so if you haven't set yours yet, you'll want to do that in your .bashrc file on Linux, or .bash_profile on OS X. For example, to define Vim as the default editor, you'd add this line to your Bash configuration:

```
export EDITOR=vim
```

Now we can create a new tmuxinator project. Let's call it "development."

---

2.   http://rvm.beginrescueend.com/

```
$ tmuxinator open development
```

This pops open the editor we assigned to the $EDITOR environment variable and displays the default project configuration, which looks like this:

scripting/default.yaml
```
project_name: Tmuxinator
project_root: ~/code/rails_project
socket_name: foo # Not needed.  Remove to use default socket
rvm: 1.9.2@rails_project
pre: sudo /etc/rc.d/mysqld start
tabs:
  - editor:
      layout: main-vertical
      panes:
        - vim
        - #empty, will just run plain bash
        - top
  - shell: git pull
  - database: rails db
  - server: rails s
  - logs: tail -f logs/development.log
  - console: rails c
  - capistrano:
  - server: ssh me@myhost
```

This is an environment that a Ruby on Rails developer who works with Git might really appreciate. This creates a tmux session with eight windows. The first window is divided into three panes, using the main-vertical layout scheme. The rest of the windows launch various servers and consoles, as you can see in Figure 11, *A Rails environment using tmuxinator's defaults*, on page 41.

As you can see, tmuxinator makes it trivial to define not only the windows and panes, but also what commands we want to execute in each one. In addition, we can specify a command we'd like to run when each window loads. Let's remove this configuration and construct our development environment, with Vim in the top window and a terminal on the bottom, starting in the ~/devproject folder:

scripting/development.yaml
```
project_name: devproject
project_root: ~/devproject
tabs:
  - editor:
      layout: main-horizontal
      panes:
        - vim
        - #empty, will just run plain bash
  - console: # empty
```

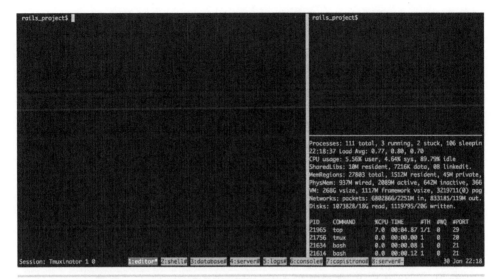

Figure 11—A Rails environment using tmuxinator's defaults

The yml file format uses two spaces for indenting, so it's really important to ensure you format the file correctly and that you don't accidentally use tabs when you write the file.

To fire up our new environment, we save the config file and then run this:

```
$ tmuxinator development
```

tmuxinator automatically loads up our original .tmux.conf file, applies our settings, and then arranges the windows and panes for us, just like we specified. If we want to make more changes to our environment, we can use

```
$ tmuxinator open development
```

again.

By default, the configuration files for tmuxinator are located in ~/.tmuxinator/, so you can find those and back them up, or share them with others.

Under the hood, tmuxinator is simply constructing a script that executes the individual tmux commands just like we did when we wrote our own script. However, it's a nicer syntax that's pretty easy to follow. It does require a Ruby interpreter on your machine though, so it may not be something you'll set up on every environment where you'd like to use tmux.

3.4 What's Next?

You can use every tmux command through the shell, which means you can write scripts to automate nearly every aspect of tmux, including running sessions. For example, you could create a keyboard binding that sources a shell script that divides the current window into two panes and logs you into your production web and database servers. We'll use that technique in Chapter 6, *Workflows*, on page 59 to force panes to open in the current directory.

We've discussed three separate ways to script out our tmux environment, and we've tinkered around with our configuration enough. We now know how to set up our projects, move around panes and windows, and launch our consoles. But as we work with applications within tmux sessions, the results of our tests or application logs start to scroll off the screen. So let's learn how to handle output buffers and how to copy and paste text.

For Future Reference

Scriptable tmux Commands

Command	Description
tmux new-session -s development -n editor	Creates a session named "development" and names the first window "editor."
tmux attach -t development	Attaches to a session named "development."
tmux send-keys -t development '[keys]' C-m	Sends the keystrokes to the "development" session's active window or pane. C-m is equivalent to pressing the ENTER key.
tmux send-keys -t development:1.1 '[keys]' C-m	Sends the keystrokes to the "development" session's first window and first pane, provided the window and pane indexes are set to 1. C-m is equivalent to pressing the ENTER key.
tmux select-window -t development:1	Selects the first window of "development," making it the active window.
tmux split-window -v -p 10 -t development	Splits the current window in the "development" session vertically, dividing it in half *horizontally* and sets its height to 10% of the total window size.
tmux select-layout -t development main-horizontal	Sets the layout for the "development" session to main-horizontal.

Command	Description
tmux -f app.conf attach	Loads the app.conf configuration file and attaches to a session created within the app.conf file.

tmuxinator Commands

Command	Description
tmuxinator open [name]	Opens the configuration file for the project name in the default text editor. Creates the configuration if it doesn't exist.
tmuxinator [name]	Loads the tmux session for the given project. Creates the session from the contents of the project's configuration file if no session currently exists, or attaches to the session.
tmuxinator list	Lists all current projects.
tmuxinator copy [source] [destination]	Copies a project configuration.
tmuxinator delete [name]	Deletes the specified project.
tmuxinator implode	Deletes all current projects.
tmuxinator doctor	Looks for problems with the tmuxinator and system configuration.

## CHAPTER 4

Working With Text and Buffers

Throughout the course of your average day, you'll copy and paste text more times than you keep track of. When you're working with tmux, you will eventually come to the point where you need to scroll backwards through the terminal's output buffer to see something that scrolled off the screen. You might also need to copy some text and paste it into a file or into another program. This chapter is all about how to manage the text inside your sessions. You'll see how to use the keyboard to scroll through tmux's output buffer, how to work with multiple paste buffers, and how to work with the system clipboard.

4.1 Scrolling Through Output with Copy Mode

When we work with programs in the Terminal, it's common that the output from these programs scrolls off the screen. But when we use tmux, we can use the keyboard to move backwards through the output buffer so we can see what we missed. This is especially useful for those times when we're running tests or watching log files.

Pressing PREFIX [places us in Copy mode. We can then use our movement keys to move our cursor around the screen. By default, the arrow keys work. But in Chapter 2, *Configuring tmux*, on page 15, we set our configuration file to use Vim keys for moving between windows and resizing panes so we wouldn't have to take our hands off the home row. tmux has a vi mode for working with the buffer as well. To enable it, add this line to .tmux.conf:

config/tmux.conf
```
setw -g mode-keys vi
```

With this option set, we can use h, j, k, and l to move around our buffer.

To get out of Copy mode, we just press the `ENTER` key. Moving around one character at a time isn't very efficient. Since we enabled vi mode, we can also use some other visible shortcuts to move around the buffer.

For example, we can use `w` to jump to the next word and `b` to jump back one word. And we can use `f`, followed by any character, to jump to that character on the same line, and `F` to jump backwards on the line.

Moving Quickly Through the Buffer

When we have several pages of buffered output, moving the cursor around to scroll isn't going to be that useful. Instead of moving word by word or character by character, we can scroll through the buffer page by page, or jump to the beginning or end of the buffer.

We can move up one page with `CTRL`-`b` and down one page with `CTRL`-`f`. We can jump all the way to the top of the buffer's history with `g`, and then jump all the way to the bottom with `G`.

Searching Through the Buffer

We don't have to browse through the hundreds of lines of content page by page if we know what we're looking for. By pressing `?` in Copy mode, we can search upwards for phrases or keywords. Simply press `?`, type in the search phrase, and press `ENTER` to jump to the first occurrence of the phrase. Then press `n` to jump to the next occurrence, or `N` to move to the previous.

To search downward, press `/` instead of `?`. Pressing `n` then jumps to the next occurrence and `N` jumps to the previous occurrence.

Learning to move around the buffer this way will dramatically speed you up. It's much faster to type the word you want to move to instead of using the arrows to move around, especially if you're looking through the output of log files.

This is just the beginning of how we can work with our buffers. Let's explore how we can copy text from one pane and paste it to another. This is Copy mode, after all.

4.2 Copying and Pasting Text

Moving around and looking for things in our output buffer is usually only half the equation. We often need to copy some text so we can do something useful with it. tmux's Copy mode gives us the opportunity to select and copy text to a paste buffer so we can dump that text elsewhere.

To copy text, we enter Copy mode and move the cursor to where we want to start selecting text. We then press `SPACE` and move the cursor to the end of the text. When we press `ENTER`, the selected text gets copied into a paste buffer.

To paste the contents we just captured, press `PREFIX` `]`.

Let's look at a few specific ways to copy and paste text from our main output buffer.

Capturing a Pane

tmux has a handy shortcut that copies the entire visible contents of a pane to a paste buffer. We simply enter Command mode with `PREFIX` `:` and type

capture-pane

We can then paste the contents into the currently focused session by using `PREFIX` `]`.

Showing and Saving the Buffer

We can display the contents of our paste buffer by using the show-buffer command, which we can execute in Command mode, or from our Terminal session with

```
$ tmux show-buffer
```

However, by using the save-buffer command, we can save the buffer to a file, which can often be a real time saver. In fact, we can capture the contents of the current pane to a text file like this:

```
$ tmux capture-pane && tmux save-buffer buffer.txt
```

or via Command mode with capture-pane; save-buffer buffer.txt. We could easily map that to a keystroke if we wanted.

Using Multiple Paste Buffers

tmux maintains a stack of paste buffers, which means we can copy text without replacing the buffer's existing content. This is much more flexible than the traditional clipboard offered by the operating system.

Every time we copy some new text, tmux creates a new paste buffer, putting the new buffer at the top of the stack. To demonstrate, let's fire up a new tmux session and load up a text editor such as Vim or Nano. In the editor, type the following sentences, one per line:

```
First sentence is first.
Next sentence is next.
Last sentence is last.
```

Now let's copy some text to the paste buffer. Enter Copy mode with PREFIX [.
Move to the start of the first sentence, press SPACE to start selecting text, move
to the end of the first sentence, and press ENTER to copy the selection. Repeat
this with the second and third sentences.

Each time we copied text, tmux created a new buffer. We can see these buffers
with the list-buffers command.

```
0: 22 bytes: "Last sentence is last."
1: 22 bytes: "Next sentence is next."
2: 24 bytes: "First sentence is first."
```

Pressing PREFIX] always pastes buffer 0, but we can issue the command choose-
buffer to select a buffer and paste the contents into the focused pane.

Split the current window in half and launch Nano in the second pane, then
enter Command mode and type this:

choose-buffer

You'll be presented with a list that looks like Figure 12, *Choosing a buffer of
text to insert*, on page 49. You can select any entry in the list, press ENTER, and
the text will be inserted into the selected pane.

This is an excellent way to manage multiple bits of text, especially in text-
based environments where you don't have access to a real clipboard.

These buffers are shared across running tmux sessions, too, so we can take
content from one session and paste it into another.

Remapping Copy and Paste Keys

If you use Vim and you'd like to make the copy and paste command keys a
little more familiar, you can remap the keys in your configuration. For
example, you can remap the ESCAPE key to switch to Copy mode, use y to "yank"
text into the buffer, use v to start Visual mode to select your text, and use p
to paste the text:

```
unbind [
bind Escape copy-mode
unbind p
bind p paste-buffer
bind -t vi-copy 'v' begin-selection
bind -t vi-copy 'y' copy-selection
```

This can be a real productivity boost if you happen to do a lot of copying and
pasting between windows and panes and are already comfortable with the
keys that Vim uses.

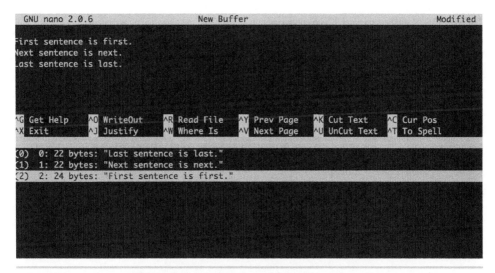

Figure 12—Choosing a buffer of text to insert

4.3 Working with the Clipboard on Linux

Using the xclip utility,[1] you can integrate your buffers with the Linux system clipboard so you can more easily copy and paste between programs.

First, you have to install xclip. On Ubuntu, use this command:

```
$ sudo apt-get install xclip
```

Then we use tmux's save-buffer and set-buffer commands with xclip.

To copy the current buffer to the system clipboard, we add this command to our .tmux.conf file:

```
bind C-c run "tmux save-buffer - | xclip -i -sel clipboard"
```

This configures PREFIX CTRL-c so it captures the current buffer and pipes its output to xclip. We then add this line to our configuration so we can use PREFIX CTRL-v to paste text from the system clipboard into a tmux session:

```
bind C-v run "tmux set-buffer \"$(xclip -o -sel clipboard)\"; tmux paste-buffer"
```

This pulls the content from xclip into a new tmux buffer and then pastes it into the selected tmux window or pane.

---

1. http://sourceforge.net/projects/xclip/

4.4 Using OS X Clipboard Commands

If you're a Mac user, you may be familiar with OS X's command-line clipboard utilities pbcopy and pbpaste. These simple utilities make it a snap to work with the clipboard. The pbcopy command captures text to the system clipboard, and the pbpaste command pastes content out. For example, you can use pbcopy and cat together to easily put the contents of your .tmux.conf file into the clipboard so you can paste it in an email or on the Web, like this:

```
$ cat ~/.tmux.conf | pbcopy
```

This is a pretty handy way to work with text, but tmux doesn't have access to these utilities, so we can't use them while running inside a tmux session. We can use a wrapper program written by Chris Johnsen to get around this limitation.[2]

To use this wrapper script, we first clone the repository and compile the wrapper.

```
$ git clone https://github.com/ChrisJohnsen/tmux-MacOSX-pasteboard.git
$ cd tmux-MacOSX-pasteboard/
$ make reattach-to-user-namespace
```

Then, we move the file to someplace on our PATH, like /usr/local/bin:

```
$ sudo mv reattach-to-user-namespace /usr/local/bin
```

Finally, we configure tmux to use the wrapper, by adding this line to .tmux.conf:

```
set -g default-command "reattach-to-user-namespace -l /bin/bash"
```

This configures the default command that tmux uses for new windows so it loads the Bash shell through the wrapper script. If you use a shell other than Bash, you'd specify its path or command instead.

Once we reload the configuration file, we'll be able to use the pbcopy command again. And as an added bonus, we can send the contents of the current tmux buffer to the system clipboard:

```
$ tmux show-buffer | pbcopy
```

Or we can paste the clipboard contents with this:

```
$ tmux set-buffer pbpaste; tmux paste-buffer
```

This means that we can also create keyboard shortcuts to do this, just like we did with Section 4.3, *Working with the Clipboard on Linux*, on page 49.

2. https://github.com/ChrisJohnsen/tmux-MacOSX-pasteboard

Unfortunately, the wrapper program we're using doesn't work with tmux's run command. The workaround is to explicitly prefix pbpaste and pbcopy with the wrapper script. So, to support copying, we'd add a binding like this:

```
bind C-c run "tmux save-buffer - | reattach-to-user-namespace pbcopy"
```

And to support pasting from the system clipboard, we'd add this longer command, which must be *all on one line*.

```
bind C-v run "tmux set-buffer \"$(reattach-to-user-namespace pbpaste)\";
tmux paste-buffer"
```

This provides a simple solution to an otherwise fairly complex technical problem.

4.5 What's Next?

By using tmux paste buffers to move text around, you gain the ability to have a clipboard in situations where you might not have one, such as when you're logged into the console of a server or without a graphical terminal. Being able to scroll back through the history of a long console output can be a huge help. It's worth installing tmux directly on your servers for that reason alone.

Now that we have a good understanding of how we move around in tmux, and we know the basics of moving from window to window and pane to pane, we can start working tmux into our daily routine. For many developers, pair programming is often part of that routine. Let's take a look at how we can use tmux to work with another developer.

For Future Reference

Shortcut Keys

Shortcut	Description
PREFIX [	Enters Copy mode.
PREFIX]	Pastes current buffer contents.
PREFIX =	Lists all paste buffers and pastes selected buffer contents.

Copy Mode Movement Keys (VI Mode)

Command	Description
h, j, k, and l	Moves the cursor left, down, up, and right, respectively.

Command	Description
w	Moves the cursor forward one word at a time.
b	Moves the cursor backward one word at a time.
f followed by any character	Moves to the next occurrence of the specified character.
F followed by any character	Moves to the previous occurrence of the specified character.
CTRL-b	Scrolls up one page.
CTRL-f	Scrolls down one page.
g	Jumps to the top of the buffer.
G	Jumps to the bottom of the buffer.
?	Starts a search backward through the buffer.
/	Starts a search forward through the buffer.

Commands

Command	Description
show-buffer	Displays current buffer contents.
capture-pane	Captures the selected pane's visible contents to a new buffer.
list-buffers	Lists all paste buffers.
choose-buffer	Shows paste buffers and pastes the contents of the one you select.
save-buffer [filename]	Saves the buffer's contents to the specified file.

## CHAPTER 5

Pair Programming with tmux

Up until now, we've spent time making configuration changes and learning how to work within tmux. But one of the most popular uses of tmux by developers is pair programming. It was actually my first introduction to tmux, and I immediately saw the potential as my friend walked me through using its various features.

Pair programming has a lot of great benefits. Working with another developer can help you see things you might not have seen on your own, but unless you're physically in the same location, pair programming can be somewhat difficult. Screen-sharing through iChat, Skype, or even GoToMeeting takes up a lot of bandwidth and can be dodgy when you're not using the best network connection. In this chapter, we'll explore using tmux for pair programming, so you can work remotely with another developer on even the slowest hotel Wi-Fi connection.

There are two ways to work with remote users. The first method involves creating a new user account that you and others share. You set up tmux and your development environment under that account and use it as a shared workspace. The second approach uses tmux's sockets so you can have a second user connect to your tmux session without having to share your user account.

Both of these methods have an inherent security flaw: they let someone else see things on your screen, and in your account. You're inviting someone in to potentially look at your files. To get around this, it's wise to use an intermediate server for pairing. Using a cheap VPS or a virtual machine with VirtualBox[1] and Vagrant[2], you can quickly create a development environment

---

1. https://www.virtualbox.org/
2. http://vagrantup.com/v1/docs/getting-started/index.html

for pairing. In this chapter, we'll be working with a remote server as we explore both of these approaches.

5.1 Pairing with a Shared Account

Using a shared account is the simplest way to work with another user. In a nutshell, you enable SSH access on the machine that will act as the host, install and configure tmux on that machine, and then create a tmux session there. The second user logs into that machine with the same user account and attaches to the session. By using SSH public keys, you can make the login process somewhat transparent. Let's walk through the setup. We'll assume we're using a server called puzzles running Ubuntu that has the SSH daemon installed.

First, we create a "tmux" user on the server. This is the user everyone will use for the pairing session.

```
tmux@puzzles$ adduser tmux
```

With the new account created, we want to configure the account so we can take SSH keys from other developers and use them to log into this account. We do this by creating the file ~/.ssh/authorized_keys under the tmux account. First, we use the su command to switch to the user:

```
tmux@puzzles$ su tmux
```

and then we create the .ssh folder and the .ssh/authorized_keys file, setting the appropriate permissions. Only the tmux user should be allowed to read, write, or execute this.

```
tmux@puzzles$ mkdir ~/.ssh
tmux@puzzles$ touch ~/.ssh/authorized_keys
tmux@puzzles$ chmod 700 ~/.ssh
tmux@puzzles$ chmod 600 ~/.ssh/authorized_keys
```

With this in place, we can transfer our keys over to the server. From our desktop machine, we take our public key and upload it to the server:

```
$ scp -p id_rsa.pub tmux@puzzles.local
```

Back on the server, we add the key to the authorized_keys file.

```
tmux@puzzles$ cat id_rsa.pub >> ~/.ssh/authorized_keys
```

We would repeat this process for any other users we wanted to share this account with.

From here, we set up tmux, text editors, compilers, programming languages, and version control systems just like we would on any other development environment. Then we can create a new tmux session on the server.

```
tmux@puzzles$ tmux new-session -s Pairing
```

Another member of our team can log in to the same machine and attach to the session with this:

```
tmux@puzzles$ tmux attach -t Pairing
```

We can then work collaboratively on our project. What's more, we can detach from the session and reattach to it later, which means we can leave our environment running for days or even weeks at a time. We'd have a persistent development environment we can log into from anywhere that has a Terminal with SSH support.

5.2 Using a Shared Account and Grouped Sessions

When two people are attached to the same tmux session, they usually both see the same thing and interact with the same windows. But there are times when it's helpful if one person can work in a different window without completely taking over control.

Using "grouped sessions," we can do just that. Let's demonstrate by creating a new session on our remote server called groupedsession.

```
tmux@puzzles$ tmux new-session -s groupedsession
```

Then, instead of attaching to the session, another user can join that session by *creating a new session* by specifying the target of the original session groupedsession and then specifying his or her *own* session name, like this:

```
tmux@puzzles$ tmux new-session -t groupedsession -s mysession
```

When the second session launches, both users can interact with the session at the same time, just as if the second user had attached to the session. However, the users can create windows independent of each other. So, if our new user creates a window, we'll both see the new window show up in the status bar, but we'll stay on the window we're currently working in! This is great for those "Hey, let me just try something" moments, or when one person wants to use Emacs and the other person prefers Vim, as in Figure 13, *Two users sharing the same session*, on page 56.

The second user can kill off his or her session with kill-session and the original will still exist. However, both sessions will be killed if all windows are closed.

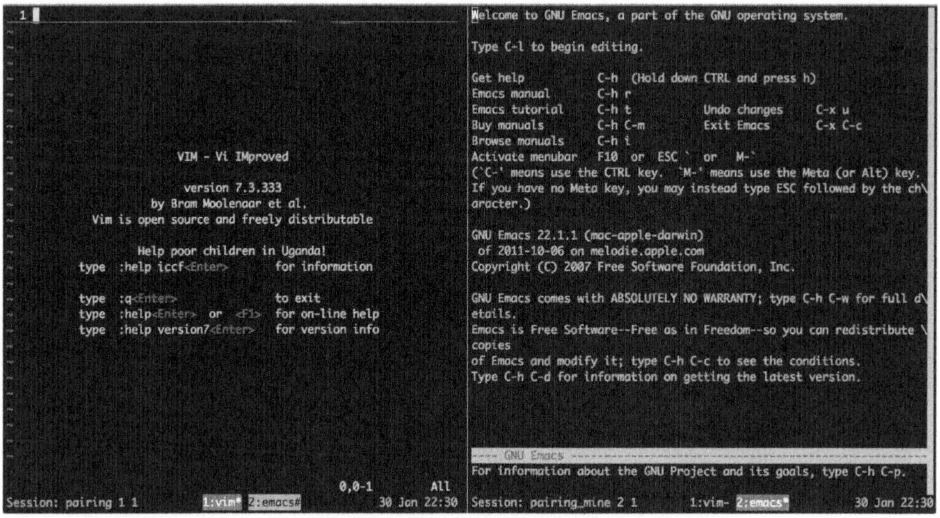

Figure 13—Two users sharing the same session

Using shared accounts and tmux is an easy way to pair, but it's not always desirable to share user accounts with team members. Let's look at an alternative approach.

5.3 Pairing with Separate Accounts and Sockets

Using tmux's support for sockets, we can create sessions that multiple users can connect to with ease.

First, let's create two new user accounts for the session: one called "ted" and another named "barney."

tmux@puzzles$ **sudo adduser ted**

tmux@puzzles$ **sudo adduser barney**

Next, we create the "tmux" group and the /var/tmux folder we'll use to hold the shared sessions.

tmux@puzzles$ **sudo addgroup tmux**

tmux@puzzles$ **sudo mkdir /var/tmux**

We change the group ownership of the /var/tmux folder so that our tmux group has access:

tmux@puzzles$ **sudo chgrp tmux /var/tmux**

Then we alter the permissions on the folder so that new files will be accessible for all members of the tmux group:

```
tmux@puzzles$ sudo chmod g+ws /var/tmux
```

Finally, we add Ted and Barney to the tmux group.

```
tmux@puzzles$ sudo usermod -aG tmux ted
```

```
tmux@puzzles$ sudo usermod -aG tmux barney
```

Creating and Sharing Sessions

Previously, we used the new-session command to create these sessions, but that uses the default socket location, which won't be reachable. Instead of creating named sessions, we create our sessions using the -S switch.

Let's log in as ted and create a new tmux session using sockets:

```
ted@puzzles$ tmux -S /var/tmux/pairing
```

In another Terminal window, we can log in as barney and then attach to the session. When we attach, we don't specify the target this time. Instead, we specify the socket and the location of the socket file, like this:

```
barney@puzzles$ tmux -S /var/tmux/pairing attach
```

The barney user now attaches to the tmux session and sees everything that the ted user sees.

It's important to note that when using this approach, the .tmux.conf file used is the one that started up the session. Having two separate accounts doesn't mean that each account gets to use its own configuration files within the tmux session, but it does mean they can customize their accounts for other purposes, and can each initiate their own tmux session as needed.

5.4   What's Next?

Now that you know how to use tmux to share your screen with others, you can use it for remote training, impromptu collaboration on open-source projects, or even presentations.

In addition, you could use this technique to fire up a tmux session on one of your production servers, load up monitoring tools or consoles, and then detach from it, leaving those tools running in the background. Then you simply connect to your machine, reattach to the session, and everything is back where you left it. I do something similar with my development environment. I set up tmux on a VPS, which lets me use nothing more than an iPad, an

SSH client, and a Bluetooth keyboard to hack on code when I'm away from home. It even works brilliantly over the 3G network.

Pair programming and working remotely are just two examples of how incorporating tmux into your workflow can make you more productive. In the next chapter, we'll look at other enhancements we can make to our environment as we explore advanced ways to work with windows, panes, and our system in general.

For Future Reference

Command	Description
tmux -S [socket]	Creates a new session using a socket instead of a name.
tmux -S [socket] attach	Attaches to an existing session using a socket instead of a name.
tmux new-session -t [existing session] -s [new session]	Creates a connection to a grouped session.

## CHAPTER 6

Workflows

By itself, tmux is just another terminal with a few bells and whistles that let us display...more terminal sessions. But tmux makes it easier to work with the programs we run in those sessions, so this chapter will explore some common, and uncommon, configurations and commands that you may find useful in your day-to-day work. You'll see some advanced ways to manage your panes and sessions, how to make tmux work with your shell of choice, how to extend tmux commands with external scripts, and how to create key-bindings that execute several commands. Let's start with windows and panes.

6.1 Working Effectively with Panes and Windows

Throughout this book, you've seen ways to divide up your tmux sessions into panes and windows. In this section, we'll look at more advanced ways to work with those panes and windows.

Turning a Pane into a Window

Panes are great for dividing up a workspace, but sometimes we need to "pop out" a pane into its own window to make reading things easier. tmux has a command to do just that.

Inside any pane, press PREFIX ! and tmux will create a new window from your pane.

Turning a Window into a Pane

Occasionally, it's nice to consolidate a workspace. We can easily take a window and turn it into a pane. To do this, we issue the join-pane command.

When we "join" a pane, we're essentially moving a pane from one session to another. We specify the source window and pane, followed by the target window and pane. If we leave the target off, the current focused window becomes the target.

To illustrate, let's create a new tmux session with two windows.

```
$ tmux new-session -s panes -n first -d
$ tmux new-window -t panes -n second
$ tmux attach -t panes
```

Now, to move the first window into a pane in the second window, we press PREFIX : to enter Command mode, and type this:

join-pane -s panes:1

This means "Take window 1 of the panes session and join it to the current window," since we didn't specify a target.

We can use this technique to move panes around as well. If our first window had two panes, we could specify the source pane like this, keeping in mind that we set our window and pane base indexes to 1 back in Chapter 2, *Configuring tmux*, on page 15.

join-pane -s panes:1.1

Here, we grab the first pane of the first window and join it to our current window.

To take it a step further, we can specify a different source session, using the notation [session_name]:[window].[pane], and we can specify a target window using the -t flag using the same notation.

Maximizing and Restoring Panes

Sometimes we just want a pane to go full-screen for a bit so we can see its contents, so we use the break-pane command. But then we have to use join-pane to put it back where it was. In tmux 1.8, the resize-pane command accepts the -Z option for zooming a pane. Best of all, it's already mapped to PREFIX z. Pressing it again restores the pane to its original size.

On tmux 1.7 and lower, zooming a pane is something we can script quite easily by using a temporary tmux window as a placeholder. Here's how.[1]

First, we'll unbind the UP arrow key so we can assign it to the new Maximize command. Then, we create a new keybinding for PREFIX UP that triggers this sequence of tmux commands:

---

1. Based on a solution from http://superuser.com/questions/238702/maximizing-a-pane-in-tmux

```
workflows/tmux.conf
unbind Up
bind Up new-window -d -n tmp \; swap-pane -s tmp.1 \; select-window -t tmp
```

This creates a new window called tmp. By giving it an explicit name, we can reference it in subsequent commands. When we create the window with the -d flag, tmux creates the window in the background rather than bringing it into focus. We then use the swap-pane command to take the pane we've selected and swap it with the pane that exists in the temporary window we created.

To restore the window, we simply use the swap-pane command to move the pane from the temporary window into the original window, select the original pane, and kill off the temporary window. We'll assign this to PREFIX DOWN, like this:

```
unbind Down
bind Down last-window \; swap-pane -s tmp.1 \; kill-window -t tmp
```

Since it uses last-window to toggle back to the original window, this approach is really intended to snap a pane full-screen and snap it back into place, but this simple hack demonstrates tmux's flexibility. We were able to automate a series of commands from a single keystroke.

Launching Commands in Panes

In Chapter 3, *Scripting Customized tmux Environments*, on page 33, we explored how to use shell commands and send-keys to launch programs in our panes, but we can execute commands automatically when we launch a window or a pane.

We have two servers, burns and smithers, which run our web server and database server respectively. When we start up tmux we want to connect to these servers using a single window with two panes.

Let's create a new script called servers.sh and create one session connecting to two servers:

```
$ tmux new-session -s servers -d "ssh deploy@burns"
$ tmux split-window -v "ssh dba@smithers"
$ tmux attach -t servers
```

When we create a new session, we can pass the command we want to execute as the last argument. In our case we fire off the new session and connect to burns in the first window, and we detach the session. Then we divide the window using a vertical split and then connect to smithers.

This configuration has a handy side effect: when we log off of our remote servers, the pane or window will close.

Issuing Commands In Many Panes Simultaneously

Every once in a while, you might need to execute the same command in multiple panes. You might need to run the same update script on two servers, for example. You can do this easily with tmux.

Using the command set-window-option synchronize-panes on, anything you type in one pane will be immediately broadcast to the other panes in the current session. Once you've issued the command, you can turn it off with set-window-option synchronize-panes on

To make this easier to do, you can map this to PREFIX CTRL-S, like this:

```
workflows/tmux.conf
bind C-s set-window-option synchronize-panes
```

By not specifying the off or on option, the synchronize-panes command acts as a toggle.

While this isn't something you'll use very often, it's amazingly handy when you need it.

6.2 Managing Sessions

As you get more comfortable with tmux, you may find yourself using more than one tmux session simultaneously. For example, you may fire up unique tmux sessions for each application you're working on so you can keep the environments contained. There are some great tmux features to make managing these sessions painless.

Moving Between Sessions

All tmux sessions on a single machine route through a single server. That means we can move effortlessly between our sessions from a single client.

To illustrate this, we'll start two detached tmux sessions, one named "editor," which launches Vim, and the other running the top command, which we'll call "processes":

```
$ tmux new -s editor -d vim
$ tmux new -s processes -d top
```

We can connect to the "editor" session with

```
$ tmux attach -t editor
```

and then we can use PREFIX (to go to the previous session and PREFIX) to move to the next session.

We can also use PREFIX s to display a list of sessions, so we can quickly navigate from one session to the next.

You can add your own custom keybindings for this to your .tmux.conf file by binding keys to the switch-client command. The default configuration looks like this:

```
bind -r ( switch-client -p
bind -r ) switch-client -n
```

If you've set up multiple workspaces, this is an extremely efficient way to move around your environments, without detaching and reattaching.

Creating or Attaching to Existing Sessions

So far, we've always taken the approach of creating new tmux sessions whenever we want to work. However, we can actually detect if a tmux session exists and connect to it if it does.

The has-session command returns a Boolean value that we can use in a shell script. That means we can do something like this in a bash script:

```
if ! tmux has-session -t development; then
  exec tmux new-session -s development -d
  # other setup commands before attaching....
fi
exec tmux attach -t development
```

If you modify the script to take a parameter, you can use this to create a single script that you can use to connect to or create any tmux session.

Moving Windows Between Sessions

We can move a window from one session to another. This is handy in case we've started up a process in one environment and want to move it around or want to consolidate our workspaces.

The move-window command is mapped to PREFIX . (the period), so we can simply bring up the window we want to move, press the key combination and then type the name of the target session.

To demonstrate, let's create two sessions, with the names "editor" and "processes," running vim and top respectively:

```
$ tmux new -s editor -d vim
$ tmux new -s processes -d top
```

We'll move the window in the "processes" session into the "editor" session.

First, we attach to the "processes" session with this:

```
$ tmux attach -t processes
```

Then, we press PREFIX . and type "editor" in the command line that appears.

This removes the only window in the "processes" session, causing it to close. If we attach to the "editor" session, we'll see both of our windows.

We can use shell commands to do this, too, so we don't need to consolidate things by opening sessions. We use move-window, like this:

```
$ tmux move-window -s processes:1 -t editor
```

Here, we're moving the first window of the "processes" session to the "editor" session.

6.3 tmux and Your Operating System

As tmux becomes part of your workflow, you may want to integrate it more tightly with your operating system. In this section, we'll show you a few ways to make tmux and your system work well together.

Using a Different Shell

In this book, we've used bash for our shell, but if you're a fan of zsh, you can still get all the tmux goodness.

We can explicitly set the default shell in .tmux.conf like this:

```
set -g default-command /bin/zsh
set -g default-shell /bin/zsh
```

Since tmux is just a Terminal multiplexer and not a shell of its own, we can just specify exactly what to run.

Launching tmux by Default

We can configure our system to launch tmux automatically when we open a Terminal. Using what we know about session names, we can create a new session if one doesn't exist.

When tmux is running, it sets the TERM variable to "screen" or the value of the default-terminal setting in the configuration file. We can use this value in our .bashrc (or .bash_profile) on OS X) file to determine whether or not we're currently in a tmux session. We set our tmux terminal to "screen-256color" back in Chapter 2, *Configuring tmux*, on page 15, so we'd use a script like this:

```
if [[ "$TERM" != "screen-256color" ]]
then
    tmux attach-session -t "$USER" || tmux new-session -s "$USER"
    exit
fi
```

If we're not already in a tmux session, we attempt to attach to one with a session name of $USER, which is our username. You can replace this with any value you want, but using the username helps avoid conflicts.

If the session doesn't exist, tmux will throw an error that the shell script can interpret as a false value. It can then run the right side of the expression, which creates a new session with our username as the session's name. It then exits out of the script.

When the tmux session starts up, it will run through our configuration file again, but this time it will see that we're in a tmux session, skip over this chunk of code, and execute the rest of the commands in our configuration file, ensuring that all our environment variables are set for us.

Now, when we create a new Terminal session, we'll be automatically attached to a session. Be careful, though, since each time you open a new Terminal window, it will be attached to the same session. Typing exit in any Terminal window will *close all the Terminal windows attached!*

Recording Program Output to a Log

Sometimes it's useful to be able to capture the output of a Terminal session to a log. We've already discussed how we can use capture-pane and save-buffer to do this, but tmux can actually record the activity in a pane right to a text file with the pipe-pane command. This is similar to the script command available in many shells, except that with pipe-pane, we can toggle it on and off at will, and we can start it after a program is already running.

To activate this, enter Command mode and type pipe-pane -o "mylog.txt".

The -o flag lets us toggle the output, which means if we send the exact command again, we can turn the logging off. To make it easier to execute this command, let's add it to our configuration script as a shortcut key.

workflows/tmux.conf
```
bind P pipe-pane -o "cat >>~/#W.log" \; display "Toggled logging to ~/#W.log"
```

Now we can press PREFIX P to toggle logging. Thanks to the display command (short for display-message), we'll see the name of the log file displayed in the status bar. The display command has access to the same variables as the status bar, which we saw in Table 1, *Status line variables*, on page 28.

Adding Battery Life to the Status Line

If you use tmux on a laptop, you may want to show the remaining battery life in your status bar, especially if you run your Terminal in full-screen mode. It turns out that this is a relatively simple thing to add thanks to the #(shell-command) variable.

Let's add the battery status to our configuration file. We'll grab a simple shell script that can fetch the remaining battery charge and place it in a file called battery in our home folder. For tmux to use the script, we have to make it executable. From our Terminal, we run these commands:

```
$ wget --no-check-certificate \
https://raw.github.com/richo/battery/master/bin/battery
```

You could also grab the battery script from the book's source code downloads.

```
$ chmod +x ~/battery
```

If we run

```
$ ~/battery Discharging
```

from the Terminal, we'll get the percentage left on the battery. We can get tmux to display this in its status bar using #(<command>). So, to display the battery in front of the clock, we change our status-right line to this:

```
set -g status-right "#(~/battery Discharging) | #[fg=cyan]%d %b %R"
```

Now, when we reload the .tmux.conf file, the battery status indicator will appear.

To get battery status when it's charging, we need to execute the command

```
$ ~/battery Charging
```

and work that into the status line. I'll leave that up to you.

You can use this approach to customize your status bar further. You'd simply need to write your own script that returns the value you want to display, and then drop it into the status bar.

6.4 What's Next?

There's so much more you can do with tmux now that you know the basics and you've had some experience playing around with various configurations. The tmux manual, which you can access from your terminal with

```
$ man tmux
```

has the complete list of configuration options and available commands.

And don't forget that tmux itself is rapidly evolving. The next version will bring new configuration options, which will give you even more flexibility.

As you integrate tmux into your workflow, you may discover other techniques you start to rely on. For example, you can use tmux and Vim together to create an incredibly effective development environment. You can even use irssi (a terminal-based IRC client) and Alpine (a terminal-based email app) within your tmux sessions, either alongside of your text editor in a pane, or in background windows. Then you can detach from the session and come back to it later, with your entire environment ready to go.

Our Configuration

Throughout the book, we've built up a somewhat complex .tmux.conf file. Here's the entire file for your reference.

workflows/tmux.conf
```
# Our .tmux.conf file

# Setting the prefix from C-b to C-a
set -g prefix C-a

# Free the original Ctrl-b prefix keybinding
unbind C-b

#setting the delay between prefix and command
set -s escape-time 1

# Ensure that we can send Ctrl-A to other apps
bind C-a send-prefix

# Set the base index for windows to 1 instead of 0
set -g base-index 1

# Set the base index for panes to 1 instead of 0
setw -g pane-base-index 1

# Reload the file with Prefix r
bind r source-file ~/.tmux.conf \; display "Reloaded!"

# splitting panes
bind | split-window -h
bind - split-window -v

# moving between panes
bind h select-pane -L
bind j select-pane -D
bind k select-pane -U
```

```
bind l select-pane -R

# Quick pane selection
bind -r C-h select-window -t :-
bind -r C-l select-window -t :+

# Pane resizing
bind -r H resize-pane -L 5
bind -r J resize-pane -D 5
bind -r K resize-pane -U 5
bind -r L resize-pane -R 5

# mouse support - set to on if you want to use the mouse
setw -g mode-mouse off
set -g mouse-select-pane off
set -g mouse-resize-pane off
set -g mouse-select-window off

# Set the default terminal mode to 256color mode
set -g default-terminal "screen-256color"

# enable activity alerts
setw -g monitor-activity on
set -g visual-activity on

# set the status line's colors
set -g status-fg white
set -g status-bg black

# set the color of the window list
setw -g window-status-fg cyan
setw -g window-status-bg default
setw -g window-status-attr dim

# set colors for the active window
setw -g window-status-current-fg white
setw -g window-status-current-bg red
setw -g window-status-current-attr bright

# pane colors
set -g pane-border-fg green
set -g pane-border-bg black
set -g pane-active-border-fg white
set -g pane-active-border-bg yellow

# Command / message line
set -g message-fg white
set -g message-bg black
set -g message-attr bright
```

```
# Status line left side
set -g status-left-length 40
set -g status-left "#[fg=green]Session: #S #[fg=yellow]#I #[fg=cyan]#P"

set -g status-utf8 on

# Status line right side
# 15% | 28 Nov 18:15
set -g status-right "#(~/battery Discharging) | #[fg=cyan]%d %b %R"

# Update the status bar every sixty seconds
set -g status-interval 60

# Center the window list
set -g status-justify centre

# enable vi keys.
setw -g mode-keys vi

# shortcut for synchronize-panes toggle
bind C-s set-window-option synchronize-panes

# Maximize and restore a pane. Only needed for 1.7 and lower.
unbind Up
bind Up new-window -d -n tmp \; swap-pane -s tmp.1 \; select-window -t tmp

unbind Down
bind Down last-window \; swap-pane -s tmp.1 \; kill-window -t tmp

# Log output to a text file on demand
bind P pipe-pane -o "cat >>~/#W.log" \; display "Toggled logging to ~/#W.log"
```

Pragmatic Guide Series

Get started quickly, with a minimum of fuss and hand-holding. The _Pragmatic Guide_ series features convenient, task-oriented two-page spreads. You'll find what you need fast, and get on with your work.

Need to learn how to wrap your head around Git, but don't need a lot of hand holding? Grab this book if you're new to Git, not to the world of programming. Git tasks displayed on two-page spreads provide all the context you need, without the extra fluff.

NEW: Part of the new _Pragmatic Guide_ series

Travis Swicegood
(160 pages) ISBN: 9781934356722. $25
http://pragprog.com/titles/pg_git

JavaScript is everywhere. It's a key component of to-day's Web—a powerful, dynamic language with a rich ecosystem of professional-grade development tools, infrastructures, frameworks, and toolkits. This book will get you up to speed quickly and painlessly with the 35 key JavaScript tasks you need to know.

NEW: Part of the new _Pragmatic Guide_ series

Christophe Porteneuve
(160 pages) ISBN: 9781934356678. $25
http://pragprog.com/titles/pg_js

The Pragmatic Bookshelf

The Pragmatic Bookshelf features books written by developers for developers. The titles continue the well-known Pragmatic Programmer style and continue to garner awards and rave reviews. As development gets more and more difficult, the Pragmatic Programmers will be there with more titles and products to help you stay on top of your game.

Visit Us Online

This Book's Home Page
http://pragprog.com/titles/bhtmux
Source code from this book, errata, and other resources. Come give us feedback, too!

Register for Updates
http://pragprog.com/updates
Be notified when updates and new books become available.

Join the Community
http://pragprog.com/community
Read our weblogs, join our online discussions, participate in our mailing list, interact with our wiki, and benefit from the experience of other Pragmatic Programmers.

New and Noteworthy
http://pragprog.com/news
Check out the latest pragmatic developments, new titles and other offerings.

Contact Us

Online Orders:	*http://pragprog.com/catalog*
Customer Service:	*support@pragprog.com*
International Rights:	*translations@pragprog.com*
Academic Use:	*academic@pragprog.com*
Write for Us:	*http://pragprog.com/write-for-us*
Or Call:	+1 800-699-7764

CPSIA information can be obtained at www.ICGtesting.com
Printed in the USA
LVOW03s2106220414

382756LV00032B/343/P